Making America Great Altogether - Call to Action

Adrian Rocquecliffe

Published by Writers Sidekick Publishing, 2024.

MAKING AMERICA GREAT ALTOGETHER - CALL TO ACTION

First edition. May 8, 2024.

ISBN: 979-8224316656

Written by Adrian Rocquecliffe.

Making America Great Altogether – Call to Action

The Call to Action, "Making America Great Altogether," underscores a crucial distinction - unity is not about everyone conforming to a single viewpoint. Instead, it advocates for a unity that celebrates the rich tapestry of perspectives that make up the nation. It promotes an inclusive unity where every voice is heard, and every perspective contributes to the collective wisdom needed to forge a better future.

At its core, this concept of unity acknowledges and embraces the diversity of ideas, beliefs, and backgrounds within American society. It recognizes that true unity does not require everyone to think or act alike; instead, it thrives on the vibrant exchange of differing viewpoints and experiences.

This vision of unity celebrates diversity, enriching the national discourse and empowering us. It fosters creativity, innovation, and resilience, inspiring us to listen to perspectives that may differ from ours, engage in meaningful dialogue, and seek common ground where possible.

In this inclusive unity, every single voice matters. Whether you're from urban centers, rural communities, different racial or ethnic backgrounds, or varied socioeconomic statuses, your perspective brings a unique insight. By ensuring that all voices are heard and valued, we tap into the collective wisdom of the nation, drawing upon a broad spectrum of experiences and knowledge to address our most pressing challenges.

This approach to unity is not just aspirational; it's a practical necessity. Drawing upon diverse perspectives and expertise is essential for navigating the increasing complexity and uncertainty challenges. By embracing inclusivity and fostering a culture of respect and openness, we build a stronger, more resilient society that can adapt and thrive in the face of adversity.

In the puzzle of progress, the Call to Action "Making America Great Altogether" promotes a vision of unity that celebrates diversity and inclusivity.

By embracing this vision, we can harness the nation's collective wisdom to create a more just, equitable, and prosperous future for all.

Perception Of The American Dream

Imagine the American Dream as this giant puzzle that people worldwide are eager to solve. It's like the ultimate challenge, promising a shiny reward at the end if you can just put all the pieces together. This dream is one of the biggest motivators for migrating to the United States. It's like hearing about this legendary puzzle that, once completed, will unlock all the opportunities and treasures you could ever imagine.

What makes this American Dream puzzle so irresistible? First, it's all about the promise of success and prosperity. Think about it like this - You've got this puzzle piece called "opportunity," and it's supposed to fit perfectly into the American Dream puzzle. People believe that in the U.S., no matter where you come from or your background, you can make something of yourself if you work hard enough. That's like the cornerstone of the American Dream - the idea that you can climb that ladder of success with enough determination and elbow grease.

Then there's the piece called "upward social mobility." Picture it as this magical piece that allows you to move on in the world when you snap it into place. There's this belief in America that you're not stuck in the same place forever. If you're willing to roll up your sleeves and hustle, you can improve your circumstances and reach for the stars. It's like having a shot at a better life, where your future isn't determined by where you started but by how hard you're willing to work.

Let's not forget about perseverance—that's another crucial puzzle piece. It's like the glue that holds the whole thing together. The American Dream isn't just about working hard; it's also about never giving up, even when things get tough. It's about picking yourself up after every setback and pushing forward, knowing that every challenge is another opportunity to prove yourself.

When people think about migrating to the United States, they're not just considering moving to a new country but taking on the ultimate puzzle-solving challenge. They're chasing that elusive American Dream, believing the key to a brighter future lies in the pieces. And that's a pretty powerful motivator, wouldn't you say?

The Concept Of The "American Dream"

The "American Dream" concept has long been ingrained in people's collective consciousness worldwide, representing the belief that the United States offers opportunities for prosperity, success, and upward social mobility through hard work, determination, and perseverance. The perception of the American Dream as a beacon of hope and opportunity has served as a powerful motivator for migration, attracting millions of immigrants and aspirants from diverse backgrounds to pursue a better life in the United States. Several key factors contribute to the enduring allure of the American Dream:

Economic Opportunity

Economic Opportunity stands as one of its most alluring pieces. It's like that golden key that unlocks the door to the American Dream, promising a shot at prosperity and success. Imagine America as this vast treasure trove, with opportunities glittering like jewels waiting to be discovered.

From the get-go, the United States has been painted as the land of plenty, where anyone with a dream and a bit of hustle can carve out their path to wealth and stability. It's like a beacon calling out to ambitious souls from across the globe, inviting them to try their luck in the world's most giant economic playground.

People flock to the U.S., lured by the promise of fat paychecks, juicy job prospects, and a buffet of goods and services that seem endless. It's like offering someone a seat at the table where the American Dream feast is served.

Whether starting your own business, coming up with the next big thing, or simply joining the workforce, America whispers sweet promises of a better life. It's the ultimate motivator, nudging folks to pack their bags and chase those dollar signs across the map.

And it's not just about making a bank. It's about securing a future for yourself and your loved ones, about having the means to live comfortably and pursue your passions. It's like having a winning ticket in the game of life, where the prize is a shot at happiness and fulfillment.

When discussing Economic Opportunity in America, we discuss more than just money. We're discussing hope, potential, and the chance to make dreams a reality. It's like a piece of the puzzle that, when placed just right, completes the picture of the American Dream.

Social Mobility

Social Mobility is like that magical bridge that connects where you start to where you want to go. It's the belief that no matter where you come from or your background, you can climb the ladder of success with enough elbow grease and determination. It's like having a secret passageway to a brighter future, beckoning those who dare to dream big.

The American Dream, at its core, is all about this idea of Social Mobility. It's about breaking free from the chains of circumstance and carving out your destiny. Imagine America as this giant playground where everyone has a fair shot at reaching for the stars.

For immigrants especially, this promise of Social Mobility is like a siren's song, calling out to those who yearn for a better life. It's like a beacon of hope in a sea of uncertainty, promising a chance to rewrite their story and legacy.

In many countries, social barriers can feel like towering walls, trapping individuals in a cycle of poverty and inequality. But in America, there's this prevailing notion that you can be the architect of your fate. It's like being handed a blank canvas and a paintbrush, with the freedom to create the life you've always wanted.

When immigrants set their sights on America, it's not just about escaping hardship. It's about chasing after the promise of Social Mobility, of reaching new heights and achieving things they never thought possible. It's like embarking on a journey where the only limits are the ones you set for yourself.

While the road to Social Mobility may be steep and winding, the idea that it's within reach for anyone willing to put in the effort keeps the American Dream alive and thriving. It's like a piece of the puzzle that, when placed just right, unlocks a world of endless possibilities.

Education And Opportunity

Education and Opportunity fit together like perfectly matched pieces, forming a pathway to success and fulfillment. Think of it as having the key to unlock countless doors of possibility, each one leading to a brighter future.

The United States boasts some of the finest educational institutions in the world, shining like beacons of knowledge and innovation. From prestigious universities to cutting-edge training programs, the American educational landscape is teeming with opportunities waiting to be seized.

For many, the allure of American education is like a magnetic force, drawing in students, professionals, and hopeful immigrants from all corners of the globe. It's like offering a front-row seat to the latest advancements in every field imaginable, with the promise of acquiring skills and expertise that can set you apart on the global stage.

But it's not just about acquiring knowledge for knowledge's sake. It's about recognizing that education is the key that unlocks the doors to lucrative careers and personal fulfillment. It's like investing in yourself, knowing that the dividends will pay off in the form of endless possibilities and newfound opportunities.

The perception of access to quality education in the U.S. is like a beacon of hope for those who dare to dream big. It's like a ladder, offering a way up for those willing to climb, regardless of their background or circumstances. Whether you're a fresh-faced student eager to soak up knowledge or a seasoned professional looking to sharpen your skills, there's a sense that America has something to offer everyone.

We discuss education and opportunity in America more thoroughly than textbooks and classrooms. We're talking about empowerment, leveling the playing field, and giving everyone a fair shot at success. It's like a piece of the puzzle that, when placed just right, unlocks a world of endless possibilities.

Freedom And Equality

Freedom and Equality are like the cornerstones that hold the whole picture together, representing the essence of the American Dream. They're like the bright colors that make the landscape vibrant, the ideals that beckon those yearning for a better, fairer world.

For many, America shines like a beacon of hope, offering sanctuary to those fleeing persecution, oppression, and discrimination in their homelands. It's like finding a safe harbor in a stormy sea, where the promise of freedom and equality feels within reach.

The United States is often seen as a shining example of democracy, where individual rights are cherished and protected by law. It's like a stage where everyone can play their part, pursue their dreams, and express their true selves without fear of reprisal.

The notion of equal treatment under the law is like a guiding principle, a North Star that guides the journey toward a more just and inclusive society. It's like offering everyone a seat at the table, regardless of their race, religion, ethnicity, gender, or sexual orientation.

While the road to true freedom and equality may be extended and fraught with challenges, the promise of America as a land of opportunity, where all are welcome and equal in the eyes of the law, keeps the dream alive.

When we talk about Freedom and Equality in America, we talk about more than lofty ideals. We're talking about the very heart and soul of the nation, the promise of a better tomorrow for all who call it home. It's like a piece of the puzzle that, when placed just right, completes the picture of the American Dream.

Cultural Influence And Global Appeal

Cultural Influence and Global Appeal are like the threads that weave together a tapestry of dreams, aspirations, and possibilities. They're like the melodies that linger in the air, the stories that capture the imagination, painting a picture of a land where anything is possible.

The American Dream has long been immortalized in literature, film, music, and popular culture, casting a spell on people far and wide. It's like a storybook coming to life, with heroes and heroines chasing after their dreams against all odds, inspiring generations to reach for the stars.

Through the magic of media, America is portrayed as a land of opportunity, innovation, and diversity, where the streets are paved with gold and dreams come true. It's like a magnet, drawing in dreamers from every corner of the globe, each one hoping to carve out their piece of the American Dream.

The image of America as a melting pot of cultures and ideas has a universal appeal that transcends borders and boundaries. It's like a language that everyone understands, a shared dream that unites people from diverse backgrounds in a common pursuit of happiness and fulfillment.

For migrants seeking to realize their dreams and aspirations, America holds a special allure, like a promised land where the sky's the limit. It's like stepping onto the world stage, with the whole world watching and cheering you on as you chase after your dreams.

When discussing Cultural Influence and Global Appeal in America, we discuss more than just movies and music. We're talking about the power of imagination, the magic of storytelling, and the universal quest for a better tomorrow. It's like a piece of the puzzle that, when placed just right, completes the picture of the American Dream.

Cultural Exports

The American Dream shines like a beacon of prosperity, freedom, and opportunity in the grand puzzle of global influence. It's like a lighthouse guiding ships through stormy seas, offering hope and inspiration to those navigating the waters of life.

Through its cultural exports—movies, television shows, music, and literature—the United States projects an image of abundance and success reverberating across continents. It's like sending out ripples in a pond, with each wave carrying the message of the American Dream to distant shores.

This dream serves as a potent form of soft power, subtly shaping perceptions of the United States and influencing the aspirations and decisions of individuals worldwide. It's like planting seeds of curiosity and desire in people's minds everywhere, sparking dreams of a better life in the land of opportunity.

Immigrants are often drawn to the allure of American culture, captivated by the promise of a better life depicted in popular media and cultural narratives. It's like being beckoned by a siren's song, lured by the promise of adventure and prosperity on distant shores.

But the influence of the American Dream goes beyond mere entertainment—it's a reflection of values deeply ingrained in the American psyche. It's like a mirror held up to the world, reflecting aspirations of freedom, equality, and the pursuit of happiness.

When we talk about global influence and soft power, we're talking about the power of dreams to transcend borders and touch people's hearts everywhere. It's like a piece of the puzzle that, when placed just right, reveals the enduring impact of the American Dream on the world stage.

Historical Legacy and Immigration

Throughout its history, the United States has been shaped by waves of immigration driven by the pursuit of the American Dream. From early European settlers seeking religious freedom to waves of immigrants arriving at Ellis Island for economic opportunity, the American Dream has driven the country's growth and development. Today, immigrants from diverse backgrounds continue to come to the United States with dreams of building a better future for themselves and their families. The legacy of past immigrants who achieved success against the odds is a source of inspiration and hope for newcomers seeking to follow in their footsteps.

Social Mobility and Economic Mobility

The American Dream encompasses the belief in social and economic mobility—the idea that individuals can improve their socioeconomic status and achieve a higher standard of living through hard work and determination. While economic disparities and social inequalities persist in the United States, the perception of upward mobility remains a powerful motivator for immigrants seeking a fresh start and better opportunities. Immigrants are often willing to take risks and make sacrifices to pursue their American Dream, believing their efforts will be rewarded with a brighter future for themselves and their families.

Family and Community Ties

For many immigrants, pursuing the American Dream is intertwined with family aspirations and community connections. Immigrants often migrate to the United States to reunite with family members who have already established roots in the country or join diaspora communities, offering support networks and opportunities for social and economic advancement. The American Dream represents the hope for a better life for oneself and future generations, with immigrants striving to create a legacy of success and prosperity for their families and communities.

Resilience and Adaptability

Despite their challenges and obstacles, immigrants are known for their resilience, resourcefulness, and adaptability in pursuing the American Dream. Immigrants bring diverse talents, skills, and experiences to the United States, contributing to the country's cultural richness, economic vitality, and innovative spirit. The American Dream embodies the belief that with perseverance and determination, individuals can overcome adversity and achieve their goals, embodying the aspirational spirit of America as a land of opportunity and possibility.

Historical Legacy And Immigration

In the grand puzzle of American history, the legacy of immigration is a defining piece, shaping the nation's very fabric. It's like tracing the footsteps of countless dreamers who crossed oceans and borders in search of a better tomorrow, each leaving an indelible mark on the story of America.

From the earliest European settlers seeking religious freedom to the waves of immigrants who passed through Ellis Island in pursuit of economic opportunity, the American Dream has been the guiding star that led them to these shores. It's like the driving force behind a great migration, fueling the hopes and aspirations of generations.

These immigrants brought their belongings and dreams—the dream of a better life, prosperity, and freedom. It's like planting seeds of ambition in the fertile soil of the New World, each one destined to grow into something greater than they could have imagined.

Today, the story continues as immigrants from every corner of the globe flock to the United States, drawn by the promise of opportunity and the chance to build a brighter future for themselves and their families. It's like a modern-day pilgrimage, with the American Dream as their guiding light.

But it's not just about the journey—it's also about the legacy left behind by those who came before. The stories of past immigrants who overcame adversity and succeeded against the odds serve as a source of inspiration and hope for newcomers following in their footsteps. It's like a torch passed from generation to generation, lighting the way for those who dare to dream.

When we talk about the historical legacy of immigration and the American Dream, we talk about more than just numbers and statistics. We're talking about the resilience of the human spirit, the power of dreams, and the enduring promise of America as a land of opportunity for all who seek it. It's like a piece of the puzzle that, when placed just right, reveals the true essence of the American Dream.

Social Mobility And Economic Mobility

In the grand puzzle of the American Dream, Social Mobility and Economic Mobility stand as twin pillars, representing the promise of a better life through hard work and perseverance. It's like the staircase to success, with each step representing an opportunity to climb higher and reach for the stars.

The belief in social and economic mobility lies at the heart of the American Dream—the idea that no matter where you start, you have the power to improve your circumstances and achieve greater prosperity. It's like having a second chance, a shot at rewriting your story and shaping your destiny.

Despite the persistent economic disparities and social inequalities in the United States, the dream of upward mobility remains a potent force, especially for immigrants seeking a fresh start and better opportunities. It's like a beacon of hope, guiding them through the challenges and uncertainties of starting anew in a foreign land.

Immigrants often arrive in the United States with little more than a dream and a willingness to work hard. They're willing to take risks and make sacrifices to pursue their American Dream, believing their efforts will be rewarded with a brighter future for themselves and their families. It's like planting hope in the fertile soil of opportunity, trusting that it will grow into something beautiful and bountiful.

And while the road to social and economic mobility may be long and arduous, the belief that it's possible—that with enough grit and determination, anything is achievable—keeps the dream alive and thriving. It's like a fire burning in the hearts of dreamers everywhere, fueling their drive to succeed against all odds.

When we talk about Social Mobility and Economic Mobility in the context of the American Dream, we're talking about more than individual success. We're talking about the promise of a better tomorrow for ourselves, our families, and our communities. It's like a piece of the puzzle that, when placed just right, completes the picture of the American Dream.

Family And Community Ties

In the grand puzzle of the American Dream, Family and Community Ties form a sturdy framework, providing support and stability as individuals navigate the journey toward a brighter future. It's like having a safety net, a foundation upon which dreams can be built and aspirations can take flight.

For many immigrants, pursuing the American Dream is not just about personal ambition—it's about reuniting with loved ones and strengthening family bonds. It's like the ties that bind, drawing people together across oceans and borders in search of a better tomorrow.

Immigrants often migrate to the United States to join family members who have already laid down roots there. It's like coming home, finding comfort and belonging in the embrace of loved ones who have paved the way for a new chapter in their lives.

But it's not just about blood relations—community connections also play a crucial role in the immigrant experience. Diaspora communities offer support networks and opportunities for social and economic advancement, serving as a lifeline for newcomers navigating the challenges of starting afresh in a foreign land.

The American Dream represents more than individual success—it's about the collective aspirations of families and communities striving for a better life together. It's like sowing seeds of hope and opportunity with the promise of a bountiful harvest for generations.

Immigrants, driven to create a legacy of success and prosperity for their families and communities, work tirelessly to turn their dreams into reality. It's like building a bridge to the future, each brick representing a step closer to a brighter tomorrow.

When we talk about Family and Community Ties in the context of the American Dream, we're talking about more than just personal goals—we're talking about the strength of the human spirit and the power of unity in the pursuit of a shared dream. It's like a piece of the puzzle that, when placed just right, completes the picture of a thriving, interconnected society built on love, resilience, and mutual support.

Resilience And Adaptability

In the grand puzzle of the American Dream, Resilience and Adaptability are shining examples of the human spirit's capacity to overcome adversity and thrive in the face of challenges. It's like the ability to bend without breaking, weather the storms of life, and emerge stronger on the other side.

Despite the myriad challenges and obstacles immigrants may encounter on their journey to pursue the American Dream, they are renowned for their resilience, resourcefulness, and adaptability. It's like having a toolkit filled with determination, ingenuity, and an unwavering belief in the power of possibility.

Immigrants bring a wealth of diverse talents, skills, and experiences, enriching the fabric of American society and contributing to its cultural richness, economic vitality, and innovative spirit. It's like adding new colors to a vibrant tapestry, each thread weaving together to create a more vibrant and dynamic whole.

But perhaps more than anything else, the American Dream embodies the belief that with perseverance and determination, anything is possible. It's like a beacon of hope in the darkest nights, guiding immigrants through the trials and tribulations of starting anew in a foreign land.

The aspirational spirit of America as a land of opportunity and possibility resonates deeply with immigrants, inspiring them to push past their limits and reach for the stars. It's like planting seeds of hope in the fertile soil of opportunity, trusting that with patience and perseverance, they will grow into something magnificent.

When we talk about Resilience and Adaptability in the context of the American Dream, we're talking about more than just individual traits—we're talking about the very essence of what it means to be American. It's like a piece of the puzzle that, when placed just right, reveals the indomitable spirit of a nation built on dreams, determination, and the relentless pursuit of a brighter tomorrow.

Entrepreneurship And Innovation

In the grand puzzle of the American Dream, Entrepreneurship and Innovation shine as beacons of opportunity, representing the boundless potential for individuals to carve out their path to success. It's like having a blank canvas and a palette of colors, with the freedom to paint your masterpiece.

The entrepreneurial spirit is closely intertwined with the American Dream—the belief that individuals can turn their ideas into successful businesses and ventures with hard work, determination, and a dash of creativity. It's like having a front-row seat to the most incredible show on Earth, where innovation and ingenuity take center stage.

Immigrants are particularly drawn to the United States because they perceive it as a fertile environment for entrepreneurship and innovation. It's like being handed the keys to a treasure trove, with access to a vibrant startup culture, ample capital, and resources to turn dreams into reality.

The American Dream represents more than just the opportunity to make a buck—it's about the chance to leave a lasting impact on society through innovation and business success. It's like planting seeds of change in the fertile soil of progress, with the potential to reshape industries, disrupt markets, and improve lives.

Entrepreneurs in America are like modern-day pioneers, blazing trails into uncharted territory and pushing the boundaries of what's possible. It's like harnessing the power of imagination to create something out of nothing, to build bridges where others see only obstacles.

When we talk about Entrepreneurship and Innovation in the context of the American Dream, we're talking about more than just business—the relentless pursuit of progress, the drive to push the envelope and redefine what it means to succeed. It's like a piece of the puzzle that, when placed just right, reveals the true essence of the American Dream as a beacon of opportunity and possibility for all who dare to dream.

Civic Engagement And Political Participation

In the grand puzzle of the American Dream, Civic Engagement and Political Participation stand as pillars of democracy, representing the power of ordinary individuals to shape the course of their nation's future. It's like having a seat at the table where decisions are made, with the opportunity to make your voice heard and your ideas count.

For immigrants, the American Dream encompasses more than just economic success—it's about active citizenship and civic engagement, fully participating in the democratic process, and contributing to the nation's political life. It's like being handed the keys to the kingdom, with the freedom to help steer the ship of state toward a brighter tomorrow.

Motivated by the opportunity to have a voice in shaping policies, advocating for their communities, and making a difference in the social and political landscape of the United States, immigrants are eager to roll up their sleeves and get involved. It's like being part of a grand experiment in democracy, where every voice and vote matter.

The American Dream represents more than just the promise of economic empowerment—it's also about political empowerment, about the ability to effect positive change through civic action and participation. It's like a torch passed from generation to generation, lighting the way for a more just and equitable society.

By engaging in the political process, immigrants strengthen their communities and enrich the tapestry of American democracy. It's like adding new colors to a painting, making each brush stroke more vibrant and dynamic.

When we talk about Civic Engagement and Political Participation in the context of the American Dream, we're talking about more than just voting and activism—it's about the fundamental belief that democracy works best when everyone has a seat at the table. It's like a piece of the puzzle that, when placed just right, reveals the true essence of American democracy as a government of the people, by the people, and for the people.

Cultural Assimilation And Integration

In the grand puzzle of the American Dream, Cultural Assimilation and Integration serve as threads that weave together the rich tapestry of American society, creating a vibrant mosaic of diverse cultures, traditions, and identities. It's like blending different colors on a canvas, creating a masterpiece celebrating diversity's beauty.

For many immigrants, the American Dream involves economic success and the aspiration to become fully integrated members of mainstream society while retaining a solid connection to their cultural heritage and identity. It's like walking a tightrope between two worlds, balancing the desire to fit in with the need to stay true to one's roots.

Immigrants aspire to embrace American values, customs, and traditions while preserving their cultural identity. It's like adding a new flavor to the melting pot of American culture, enriching it with the unique perspectives and experiences of people from around the world.

The American Dream represents the ideal of a melting pot or mosaic society. Diversity is tolerated and celebrated in this place, where individuals from different backgrounds come together to form a cohesive and inclusive community. It's like a symphony of many voices, each contributing its melody to create a harmonious whole.

Cultural assimilation and integration are not about erasing differences but finding common ground and building bridges of understanding and respect. It's like building a quilt, stitching together different fabrics to create something beautiful and unified.

When we talk about Cultural Assimilation and Integration in the context of the American Dream, we're talking about more than just blending in—we're talking about finding belonging and acceptance while honoring the richness of our diverse heritage. It's like a piece of the puzzle that, when placed just right, reveals the true beauty of America as a land where unity is found in diversity.

Personal Fulfillment And Self-Actualization

In the grand puzzle of the American Dream, Personal Fulfillment and Self-Actualization are the pieces that complete the picture of a life well-lived—a journey toward happiness, fulfillment, and the realization of one's true potential. It's like finding the missing piece of the puzzle that completes the picture of a life filled with purpose and meaning.

At its core, the American Dream is about more than just material success—the pursuit of personal fulfillment and self-actualization, the quest to live a deeply satisfying and meaningful life. It's like embarking on a journey of self-discovery, where each step brings you closer to uncovering your true purpose and passion.

Immigrants are drawn to the United States by the promise of personal freedom, autonomy, and the opportunity to pursue their passions, interests, and aspirations. It's like being handed a blank canvas and a paintbrush, with the freedom to create the life you've always imagined.

The American Dream represents the belief that individuals can define their paths, chart their destinies, and live life to the fullest, regardless of their background or circumstances. It's like having the power to write your story, shape your destiny, and make your mark on the world.

But personal fulfillment and self-actualization are not just about individual happiness—they're also about contributing to the greater good and positively impacting the world. It's like finding fulfillment not only in achieving our own goals but also in helping others achieve theirs.

When we talk about Personal Fulfillment and Self-Actualization in the context of the American Dream, we're talking about more than just personal success—we're talking about the pursuit of a life that is rich in meaning, purpose, and fulfillment. It's like a piece of the puzzle that, when placed just right, reveals the true essence of the American Dream as a journey toward a life well-lived.

Legacy And Generational Progress

In the grand puzzle of the American Dream, Legacy and Generational Progress are like the threads that bind the past, present, and future together, weaving a narrative of hope, perseverance, and resilience. It's like planting seeds today, believing they will grow into mighty trees, providing shade and sustenance for generations.

At its heart, the American Dream often involves the desire to leave behind a legacy of success and progress for future generations. Immigrants, in particular, come to the United States with dreams for themselves and their children and grandchildren. It's like setting sail toward a better tomorrow, guided by the North Star of opportunity and possibility.

The American Dream represents more than individual aspirations—it's about the collective hope of upward mobility and intergenerational progress. Each generation strives to build upon the achievements of those who came before them, paving the way for future success and prosperity. It's like passing the baton in a relay race, with each runner pushing themselves to go farther and faster than the one before.

Immigrants often sacrifice and work tirelessly to provide their families with better opportunities and a brighter future. It's like laying the foundation for a sturdy house, with each brick representing the hopes and dreams of those who came before.

But the legacy of the American Dream is not just about material success—it's also about instilling values of hard work, resilience, and perseverance in future generations. It's like passing down a torch of hope and possibility, lighting the way for those who follow in our footsteps.

When we talk about Legacy and Generational Progress in the context of the American Dream, we're talking about more than just individual achievements—we're talking about the enduring impact of our collective efforts to build a better tomorrow for ourselves and for those who come after us. It's like a piece of the puzzle that, when placed just right, reveals the true essence of the American Dream as a journey toward a brighter future for all.

There Is Hope

Indeed, the American Dream is often portrayed as an ideal—a vision of boundless opportunity, upward mobility, and personal fulfillment. But the reality is far more complex. In a country marked by deep divisions, systemic inequalities, and social injustices, the dream can often feel like just that—a dream rather than a tangible reality.

The challenges highlighted—religious biases, political discord, discrimination, and the decline of education, arts, and cultural integration—are indeed significant barriers to realizing the American Dream for many people. These issues hinder individual progress and undermine society's collective fabric, eroding trust, unity, and social cohesion.

In a society where access to opportunity is not evenly distributed, where systemic barriers persist, and where certain groups face discrimination and marginalization, the American Dream can seem like an illusion. This promise remains out of reach for far too many.

But despite these challenges, there is hope. The fact that we can acknowledge and confront these issues is a testament to the resilience and strength of the American spirit. By working together to address systemic injustices, promote equality and inclusivity, and build a more just and equitable society, we can begin to bridge the gap between the dream and reality.

It's essential to recognize that the American Dream is not a static concept—it evolves and is shaped by each generation's collective actions and aspirations. By challenging the status quo, advocating for change, and actively participating in civic life, we can move closer to realizing the promise of the American Dream for all.

Ultimately, it's up to us—as individuals, as communities, and as a nation—to confront the harsh realities that stand in the way of the American Dream and to work together to build a future where that dream is accessible to all, not just a select few. It's a daunting task, but it is essential to truly live up to the ideals upon which this nation was founded.

The Current State Of America

The perception of the greatness of the United States of America is subjective. It varies among individuals based on their experiences, perspectives, and values. The notion of greatness is often intertwined with a country's achievements, cultural influence, economic power, and democratic ideals. Here are some aspects to consider when evaluating the perception of the United States:

Cultural And Technological Influence

Imagine culture and technology as two pieces of a giant puzzle, and the United States is the master puzzler who keeps adding new pieces. Regarding culture, think of America as this vibrant canvas splashed with colors from all over the world. Music? Yeah, the U.S. has given us jazz, blues, rock, hip-hop - a whole jukebox of genres. Films? Hollywood is like the blockbuster factory that churns out movies everyone wants to watch, from heartwarming tales to mind-bending sci-fi flicks.

But wait, there's more! Technology is another piece of this puzzle, and boy, has the U.S. been busy, and have you ever heard of the internet? American ingenuity brought that to life, forever changing how we connect and share information. And let's not forget about Silicon Valley. Innovations like smartphones, social media, and gadgets are in this techie paradise.

Why does this matter? These cultural and technological contributions aren't just fantastic bragging rights for America. They've shaped the global landscape, influencing how people worldwide listen to music, watch movies, communicate, and even live their daily lives. In a way, the U.S. is like the puzzle whiz that keeps adding pieces to the ever-evolving picture of global culture and technology.

Economic Power

Picture the economy as another piece of this grand puzzle, and the U.S. is like the puzzle piece that's not just big but shiny and loaded with cash. It's like having the jackpot piece in Monopoly!

What makes the U.S. economy so powerful? Well, for starters, it's got its fingers dipped in all sorts of pies. Many industries drive the economy forward, from tech giants in Silicon Valley to Wall Street's financial wizards. You've got classic sectors like manufacturing, agriculture, and cutting-edge stuff like biotech and renewable energy.

And let's not forget about the big players in the financial world. Wall Street is like the financial nerve center of the universe, where stocks are traded, fortunes are made (and sometimes lost), and the economy's heartbeat is felt.

But what does all this mean for everyday folks? Well, the U.S. economy's strength translates into a high standard of living for many Americans. It means more job opportunities, better wages, and much stuff on the shelves at your local store. When you think about it, the U.S. economy isn't just a puzzle piece; it's more like the glue holding the whole puzzle together, ensuring everything runs smoothly and everyone gets a fair slice of the pie.

Democratic Values

Imagine democratic values as the golden thread woven throughout the fabric of American society, holding everything together like a sturdy safety net. In the governance puzzle, the United States proudly displays its democratic values as the centerpiece.

What exactly are these democratic principles all about? Well, think of them as the guiding lights that steer the ship of the nation. At the heart of it all is the Constitution, that grand blueprint for how the country should run. It's like the rulebook everyone agrees to play by, ensuring no person or group gets too much power.

And then there's the Bill of Rights, which is like a set of supercharged power-ups for individual freedoms. It's got everything from freedom of speech and religion to the right to bear arms and a fair trial. These rights aren't just fancy words on paper; they're the backbone of American democracy, ensuring every citizen has a voice and a say in how things are run.

But it's not just about the rules but the spirit behind them. American democracy is all about inclusivity, equality, and respect for diversity. It's about recognizing that everyone deserves a seat at the table, no matter their background or beliefs.

When you think about democratic values in the U.S., think of them as the glue that binds the nation together, ensuring everyone has a chance to thrive and contribute to the ever-expanding puzzle of American society.

Educational And Research Institutions

Think of educational and research institutions in the U.S. as the powerhouse behind the scenes, quietly fueling the engine of progress and innovation. In the puzzle of knowledge and discovery, these institutions are the pieces that fit snugly into place, pushing boundaries and unlocking new horizons.

First off, let's talk about universities. The U.S. is like the Ivy League capital of the world, with prestigious institutions like Harvard, MIT, and Stanford leading the pack. But it's not just about fancy degrees and ivy-covered walls; these universities are hotbeds of research and creativity, where brilliant minds come together to tackle humanity's toughest challenges.

Then, there are research institutions like NASA, the National Institutes of Health, and the Department of Energy's national labs. These are the places where scientists and engineers dream big and make those dreams a reality. Whether it's exploring outer space, curing diseases, or developing clean energy technologies, these institutions are at the forefront of cutting-edge research and innovation.

But what makes these institutions so attractive to scholars and professionals worldwide? Well, it's not just the top-notch facilities or the world-class faculty (although those are big draws). It's also a culture of collaboration and openness to new ideas. In the U.S., innovation thrives on diversity and exchange, and these institutions are like melting pots where people from all backgrounds come together to learn, discover, and create.

When you think about educational and research institutions in the U.S., consider them the secret sauce that makes the American dream possible. They're the engines of progress, driving society forward one breakthrough at a time and adding yet another piece to the ever-expanding puzzle of human knowledge.

Cultural Diversity

Imagine cultural diversity as a kaleidoscope of colors, each shade representing a different culture, tradition, and perspective. In the grand puzzle of society, the United States proudly showcases its cultural diversity as one of its most vibrant and captivating pieces.

What exactly makes the U.S. so culturally diverse? Well, it's like a giant melting pot where people from all corners of the globe come together to create something beautiful. Whether it's the bustling streets of New York City or the quiet towns of the Midwest, you'll find a rich tapestry of languages, cuisines, and customs that reflect the incredible diversity of the American population.

But it's not just about the mix of cultures; it's about how they create something more significant than the sum of their parts. In the U.S., cultural diversity isn't just a buzzword; it's a way of life. It's about celebrating differences, embracing new experiences, and learning from one another.

And let's not forget about the immigrants. The U.S. has been a beacon of hope for people seeking a better life for centuries. From the early settlers to the millions of immigrants who arrive on its shores each year, the U.S. has welcomed people from all walks of life with open arms, allowing them to chase their dreams and contribute to the rich tapestry of American society.

When you think about cultural diversity in the U.S., think of it as the spice that adds flavor to the American experience. It's what makes the country so unique, so vibrant, and so endlessly fascinating. In the puzzle of society, cultural diversity isn't just a piece; it's the glue that holds the whole thing together, reminding us that we're all part of something bigger than ourselves.

Challenges And Criticisms

Imagine the challenges and criticisms facing the United States as the storm clouds on an otherwise sunny day, casting shadows over the landscape of progress. In the puzzle of society, these challenges are like stubborn pieces that won't seem to fit, reminding us that the picture isn't always perfect.

First off, let's talk about racial inequality. Despite strides towards equality, the U.S. still grapples with deep-rooted issues of systemic racism and discrimination. From disparities in education and employment to unequal treatment by law enforcement, racial inequality continues to cast a long shadow over American society, sparking protests and calls for change.

Then there are economic disparities. While the U.S. boasts a booming economy, not everyone is reaping the benefits. Income inequality is rising, with the gap between the rich and the poor widening yearly. This leaves many Americans struggling to make ends meet, unable to access the same opportunities for success as their wealthier counterparts.

And let's not forget about healthcare access. While the U.S. is home to some of the world's top medical facilities, millions of Americans still lack access to affordable healthcare. This leaves them vulnerable to illness and financial ruin, sparking debates over healthcare reform and the role of government in ensuring access to care for all.

Finally, there's political polarization. Bipartisan cooperation seems like a distant dream in an increasingly divided political landscape. Instead, the U.S. is gripped by partisan gridlock, with politicians more focused on scoring points against their opponents than finding solutions to the nation's pressing problems.

But here's the thing—challenges and criticisms are a natural part of any society's evolution. They're like bumps that remind us to stay vigilant and keep pushing forward. In the puzzle of society, it's not just about fitting all the pieces together perfectly; it's about facing the challenges head-on, learning from our mistakes, and working together to create a brighter future for all.

Global Leadership And Responsibility

Think of global leadership and responsibility as the United States stepping onto the world stage with a megaphone ready to make its voice heard and make a difference. In the puzzle of global affairs, the U.S. is like the puzzle piece that's front and center, shaping the picture of international relations.

What exactly does global leadership entail? For starters, it's about being a team player in the global community. The U.S. is a critical player in international organizations like the United Nations, NATO, and the World Bank, working alongside other nations to tackle pressing issues like climate change, poverty, and global health.

But it's not just about sitting at the table; it's about leading by example. The U.S. is known for its generous foreign aid programs, which assist countries in need and help promote stability and development worldwide. Whether it's disaster relief, humanitarian assistance, or economic development projects, the U.S. is often at the forefront of global efforts to alleviate suffering and improve lives.

And let's not forget about peacekeeping efforts. From maintaining peace in war-torn regions to combating terrorism and piracy, the U.S. military plays a crucial role in promoting stability and security on the world stage.

But here's where the debates come in. While many applaud the U.S. for its global leadership and generosity, others question the nature of its influence. Some argue that the U.S. acts in its interests rather than the greater good. In contrast, others criticize its military interventions and foreign policy decisions.

But regardless of where you stand on the issue, one thing's for sure - global leadership and responsibility are like the threads that weave together the fabric of international relations. In the puzzle of global affairs, the U.S. is like the guiding hand that helps shape the picture of a safer, more prosperous world for all.

Social And Political Issues

Imagine social and political issues as the rocky terrain in American society's journey, full of twists, turns, and unexpected obstacles. These issues are like tricky pieces in the governance puzzle that require careful maneuvering and collaboration to fit into place.

First, let's discuss social issues. From debates over gun control and immigration to discussions about LGBTQ+ rights and racial justice, the United States is a hotbed of passionate discourse on various social issues. These debates reflect the diverse perspectives and values held by Americans across the country. However, they also highlight the deep divisions that exist within society.

Then there are the political divisions. In an era of increasingly polarized politics, finding common ground seems like an uphill battle. Democrats and Republicans often find themselves at loggerheads, unable to bridge the gap between their competing ideologies. This gridlock can make it challenging to address pressing issues and find solutions that benefit all Americans.

Let's not forget the challenges in healthcare, education, and infrastructure. Despite being a wealthy and developed nation, the United States still struggles with issues like access to affordable healthcare, disparities in educational opportunities, and crumbling infrastructure. These challenges impact Americans' daily lives and undermine the country's ability to compete on the global stage.

But here's the thing - social and political issues aren't just roadblocks but also opportunities for growth and progress. By engaging in open dialogue, fostering empathy, and seeking common ground, Americans can work together to address these complex challenges and build a better future for all.

The Perception Of Greatness

Social and political issues are like the pieces that test our patience and resilience in the puzzle of American society. But with determination and cooperation, we can fit them into place and create a more equitable and prosperous nation for generations.

It's essential to recognize that perceptions of greatness can coexist with critiques and recognition of areas that require improvement. People's views of the U.S. may be shaped by personal experiences, cultural backgrounds, and the lens through which they interpret historical and contemporary events.

Ultimately, whether the United States is as great as people make it to be is subjective and depends on individual perspectives, values, and priorities. Celebrating achievements, acknowledging challenges, and fostering constructive dialogue are essential for a nuanced understanding of any country.

Overview Of Critical Challenges And Issues

The current state of America is marked by a complex tapestry of critical challenges and issues that demand thoughtful examination and proactive solutions. As we navigate the intricate landscape of the nation, it becomes evident that specific key challenges are at the forefront, shaping the socio-political and economic fabric of the country.

Socio-Economic Inequality

Imagine socio-economic inequality as a deep chasm separating different segments of American society, with some standing on the sunny side of opportunity. In contrast, others languish in the shadows of disadvantage. In the puzzle of social justice, this challenge is like the stubborn piece that won't seem to fit, casting a long shadow over the promise of equal opportunity.

First, let's discuss the widening gap between the wealthy and the economically disadvantaged. While the United States boasts tremendous wealth and prosperity, not everyone is reaping the benefits. Instead, the gap between the haves and the have-nots has grown more expansive, leaving many Americans struggling to make ends meet while others enjoy lavish lifestyles.

This disparity in wealth translates into disparities in access to essential services like education, healthcare, and employment opportunities. For example, economically disadvantaged communities often lack access to quality schools and resources, making them disadvantaged early on. Similarly, limited access to affordable healthcare can leave individuals and families vulnerable to illness and financial ruin, further perpetuating the cycle of poverty.

However, perhaps the most troubling issue is the impact of economic inequality on the essence of equal opportunity that America strives to uphold. In a society where factors like wealth and social status often determine success, the promise of equal opportunity begins to ring hollow. Instead of a level playing field where everyone has a fair shot at success, we see barriers and obstacles that make it harder for some to achieve their dreams.

But here's the thing - socio-economic inequality isn't just a moral issue; it's also an economic one. When large segments of the population are left behind, it weakens the fabric of society and undermines the country's overall prosperity. That's why addressing this challenge isn't just the right thing to do; it's also essential for the long-term health and well-being of the nation.

In the puzzle of American society, socio-economic inequality is like the puzzle piece that demands our attention and action. By working together to dismantle barriers and create a more equitable society, we can ensure that every American has the opportunity to thrive and succeed, regardless of their background or circumstances.

Healthcare

Imagine the healthcare system as a labyrinthine maze, with millions of Americans navigating its twists and turns in search of essential medical care. This challenge is like the missing piece in the public health puzzle, leaving gaps in the picture of a society that cares for its citizens' well-being.

First off, let's talk about accessibility and affordability. While the United States boasts some of the world's most advanced medical facilities and treatments, not everyone has equal access to healthcare. Millions of Americans face barriers to essential medical services and medications, whether due to lack of insurance, high out-of-pocket costs, or limited availability of healthcare providers in their communities.

The complexities of the healthcare system itself compound these challenges. From navigating insurance plans and billing procedures to deciphering medical jargon and treatment options, many Americans find themselves overwhelmed by the sheer complexity of the system. This can lead to delays in seeking care, inadequate treatment, and unnecessary suffering for those in need.

However, perhaps the most troubling factor is the human cost of these challenges. For many Americans, access to healthcare isn't just a matter of convenience; it's a matter of life and death. Without timely and affordable access to medical care, individuals and families are left vulnerable to illness, injury, and chronic conditions that can have devastating consequences for their health and well-being.

Addressing these issues is paramount to ensuring the well-being of the nation's citizens and fostering a healthcare system that leaves no one behind. It's about recognizing that access to healthcare is a fundamental human right and taking concrete steps to make that right a reality for all Americans.

In the puzzle of public health, addressing healthcare accessibility and affordability is like finding the missing piece that completes the picture of a society that values the health and well-being of all its citizens. By working together to dismantle barriers and create a more equitable healthcare system, we can ensure that every American has the opportunity to lead a healthy and fulfilling life.

Environmental Concerns

Imagine the country's future as a delicate ecosystem, with environmental concerns looming like dark clouds on the horizon. This challenge is like the missing piece in the sustainability puzzle that threatens to disrupt the delicate balance between economic growth and environmental preservation.

First off, let's talk about climate change. It's like the elephant in the room, impossible to ignore and urgent to address. With each passing year, extreme weather events like hurricanes, wildfires, and droughts are becoming more frequent and severe, wreaking havoc on communities and ecosystems nationwide. The need for action has never been more pressing as we face the genuine threat of irreversible damage to our planet's climate system.

But it's not just about the big-picture stuff; it's also about everyday practices and habits contributing to environmental degradation. From carbon emissions and pollution to deforestation and habitat destruction, human activities are destroying the planet's natural resources and biodiversity. If left unchecked, these trends could have far-reaching consequences for future generations.

Finding a solution to these challenges requires delicate navigation. On the one hand, there's the imperative of economic growth and development, which fuels prosperity and improves the quality of life for millions of Americans. On the other hand, there's the need for environmental preservation, which ensures that future generations can enjoy clean air, clean water, and a healthy planet.

But here's the thing—economic growth and environmental preservation don't have to be mutually exclusive. They can go hand in hand. We can create a future where economic prosperity and environmental stewardship are mutually exclusive by embracing sustainable practices and investing in renewable energy, clean technology, and conservation efforts.

In the sustainability puzzle, addressing environmental concerns is like finding the missing piece that completes the picture of a prosperous and sustainable future. By working together to find innovative solutions and embrace sustainable practices, we can ensure a harmonious coexistence with the planet for future generations.

Social And Racial Tensions

Imagine social and racial tensions as cracks in the foundation of American society, threatening to widen and deepen unless addressed with urgency and resolve. In the puzzle of social justice, this challenge is like the missing piece that prevents the picture of a truly equitable and inclusive society from coming into focus.

First, discuss the deep-seated inequalities and systemic injustices affecting marginalized communities. From disparities in education and employment to disproportionate rates of poverty and incarceration, these injustices are woven into the fabric of American society, perpetuating cycles of disadvantage and exclusion.

At the heart of these inequalities lie issues of race and ethnicity. For centuries, people of color in the United States have faced discrimination and oppression, from slavery and segregation to racial profiling and police brutality. While progress has been made in some areas, the legacy of racism and systemic racism continues to cast a long shadow over the lives of millions of Americans.

Addressing these issues requires a profound reckoning with the nation's history and a commitment to creating a more equitable and inclusive society. It's about acknowledging the injustices of the past and working to dismantle the systems and structures that perpetuate inequality and discrimination in the present.

But it's not just about policy changes and institutional reforms; it's also about changing hearts and minds. It's about fostering empathy and understanding across racial and cultural lines and recognizing the humanity and dignity of all people, regardless of race, ethnicity, or background.

In the puzzle of social justice, addressing social and racial tensions is like finding the missing piece that completes the picture of a society where every individual is valued and respected. All have equal opportunities to thrive and succeed. By confronting these challenges head-on and working together to build a more just and equitable future, we can create a society that lives up to the ideals of equality and justice for all.

Understanding The Interconnectedness

Imagine the challenges facing America as a tangled web, with each thread interconnected and woven into the fabric of society. Understanding this interconnectedness in the progress puzzle is like finding the key that unlocks the path to sustainable change.

First and foremost, it's crucial to recognize that these challenges are not isolated; they're deeply intertwined. Issues like socio-economic inequality, healthcare access, environmental sustainability, and social and racial tensions don't exist in a vacuum. Instead, they feed off each other, exacerbating existing disparities and creating a cycle of injustice and hardship for many Americans.

That's where a holistic approach comes in. Rather than just treating the symptoms, we must address the root causes of these issues. This means digging deep to understand the historical context that has shaped the current landscape and acknowledging the systemic factors perpetuating inequality and injustice. It also means recognizing that solutions to these challenges must be comprehensive, simultaneously tackling multiple facets of the problem.

Enter "Making America Great Altogether." This Call to Action seeks to unravel the complexities of America's multifaceted challenges, providing insights into the historical forces that have shaped the current landscape while advocating for comprehensive solutions. By examining the interconnectedness of issues like socio-economic inequality, healthcare access, environmental sustainability, and social and racial tensions, Making America Great Altogether offers a roadmap for sustainable progress.

But it's not just about understanding; it's also about action. "Making America Great Altogether" calls on readers to become agents of change, advocating for policies and practices that promote equity, justice, and inclusivity. It's about recognizing that we all have a role in building a better future for ourselves and future generations.

In the puzzle of progress, "Making America Great Altogether" is like the guidebook that helps us navigate the complexities of our nation's challenges and chart a course toward a more just, equitable, and sustainable future. By embracing a holistic approach and working together to address root causes, we can truly make America great for all.

Navigating The Current State Of America

Navigating America's current state is like embarking on a complex journey through uncharted territory. To navigate successfully, we need more than just a map; we need a nuanced understanding of the challenges. This means acknowledging the interplay between various issues and devising strategies that foster inclusive growth.

First and foremost, it's essential to recognize that these challenges are interconnected. Issues like socio-economic inequality, healthcare access, environmental sustainability, and social and racial tensions are not standalone problems; they are deeply intertwined, each influencing and exacerbating the others. Understanding this interconnectedness is critical to devising effective solutions that address the root causes rather than just treating the symptoms.

As we confront these challenges head-on, adopting a mindset of inclusivity is important. This means ensuring that our strategies for progress benefit all members of society, regardless of race, ethnicity, gender, or socioeconomic status. Inclusive growth isn't just about boosting GDP or increasing productivity; it's about creating opportunities for everyone to thrive and succeed, leaving no one behind.

The journey towards a stronger and more united America begins with thoroughly examining the critical challenges that define our present reality. This means taking stock of where we are, how we got here, and where we want to go. It means acknowledging past injustices and committing to building a more just, equitable, and inclusive future for all.

But this journey won't be easy. It will require courage, determination, and a willingness to confront uncomfortable truths. We must listen to diverse perspectives, engage in difficult conversations, and challenge the status quo. Ultimately, it's worth taking because it's a journey towards a better America.

In the puzzle of progress, navigating America's current state requires us to embrace complexity, acknowledge interdependence, and work together to build a brighter future. By confronting our challenges with humility and empathy, we can chart a course toward a stronger, more united, and more inclusive America for generations to come.

The Reality of the Greatness of America

While the U.S. has achieved significant successes, some criticisms and concerns contribute to a more nuanced view of the country's greatness. Here are some reasons why some people may hold the perspective that the United States falls short of its perceived greatness:

Social Inequality

Social inequality in the United States is a deeply ingrained and pervasive issue that persists despite the nation's status as one of the wealthiest in the world. This inequality manifests in profound socio-economic disparities that affect millions of Americans, exacerbating divisions and undermining the principles of equality and fairness upon which the country was founded.

The widening gap between the affluent and the economically disadvantaged is at the heart of social inequality. While some Americans enjoy unprecedented wealth and privilege, millions struggle to make ends meet, trapped in cycles of poverty and limited opportunity. This disparity in wealth and income translates into unequal access to essential resources and services, including education, healthcare, and opportunities for upward mobility.

Education, often hailed as the great equalizer, remains out of reach for many disadvantaged communities. Underfunded schools, overcrowded classrooms, and inadequate resources perpetuate educational inequalities, limiting the life chances of students from low-income backgrounds. As a result, the promise of upward mobility through education becomes increasingly elusive for those trapped in poverty.

Similarly, access to healthcare is unequal in the United States, with millions of Americans lacking affordable coverage and facing barriers to essential medical services. Racial and ethnic minorities, in particular, experience disparities in healthcare outcomes stemming from systemic biases and discrimination within the healthcare system. These disparities contribute to poorer health outcomes and perpetuate cycles of poverty and inequality.

Persistent issues like racial discrimination and gender inequality further compound social divisions and exacerbate disparities. Systemic injustices, such as racial profiling, discriminatory hiring practices, and unequal treatment under the law, undermine the notion of equality and fairness, perpetuating social inequality and eroding trust in institutions.

Moreover, social inequality has far-reaching consequences, undermining social cohesion and economic stability. Widening income inequality contributes to social unrest and political polarization, threatening the fabric of democracy and exacerbating social tensions.

Addressing social inequality requires a multifaceted approach that addresses its root causes and promotes equity and justice for all Americans. This includes investing in education and healthcare, implementing policies that promote economic opportunity and social mobility, and combating discrimination and systemic biases in all their forms. By working together to dismantle barriers and promote inclusivity, we can create a society where every individual has the opportunity to thrive and succeed, regardless of their background or circumstances.

Economic Challenges

Despite its reputation for having a robust economy, the United States contends with several economic challenges that cast doubt on its perceived greatness. These issues contribute to a sense of unease and dissatisfaction among many Americans, revealing systemic flaws in the economic system that undermine notions of prosperity and economic security for all citizens.

One of the most pressing economic challenges is stagnant wages, which have failed to keep pace with the rising cost of living. Despite increases in worker productivity and corporate profits, wages for many Americans have remained relatively flat, leading to a decline in purchasing power and living standards. This trend has contributed to growing income inequality, with the wealthiest individuals and corporations capturing an increasingly disproportionate share of economic gains.

Rising income inequality is another primary concern, highlighting disparities in wealth and opportunity across society. As the gap between the rich and the poor widens, the middle class faces increasing economic insecurity and downward mobility. This erosion of the middle class, once a cornerstone of American prosperity, threatens social stability and economic vitality.

Furthermore, concerns about job insecurity weigh heavily on the minds of many Americans, particularly in the face of automation, globalization, and technological advancements that disrupt traditional industries and occupations. The rise of precarious employment, characterized by part-time work, gig economy jobs, and contingent labor arrangements, has left many workers vulnerable to economic shocks and instability.

Access to affordable housing is another significant economic challenge, particularly in urban areas where housing costs have skyrocketed, outpacing wage growth and exacerbating housing affordability crises. Many Americans struggle to find affordable and stable housing, leading to homelessness, overcrowding, and housing instability.

Additionally, mounting student debt has emerged as a significant barrier to economic mobility and prosperity for millions of Americans. The soaring cost of higher education, with stagnant wages and limited job opportunities for recent graduates, has left many young adults saddled with crushing levels of student loan debt, hindering their ability to save, invest, and achieve financial independence.

In conclusion, while the United States may boast a strong economy on the surface, it faces several economic challenges that undermine perceptions of greatness and prosperity. Issues such as stagnant wages, rising income inequality, job insecurity, lack of affordable housing, and mounting student debt highlight systemic flaws in the economic system that must be addressed to ensure shared prosperity and economic security for all citizens. Addressing these challenges requires bold and comprehensive solutions that promote inclusive growth, expand economic opportunity, and safeguard the well-being of all Americans.

Healthcare Accessibility

Despite being one of the wealthiest nations globally, the United States has significant challenges in providing affordable and accessible healthcare to all its citizens. The healthcare system's high cost and disparities in coverage and outcomes leave millions without adequate access to essential services. This glaring deficiency undermines the well-being of Americans. It raises questions about the nation's commitment to the welfare of its people.

One of the most prominent challenges in healthcare accessibility is the high cost of medical care. Healthcare expenses in the United States are among the highest in the world, with costs continuing to rise at a rate outpacing inflation and wage growth. As a result, many Americans struggle to afford necessary medical services, medications, and treatments, leading to financial hardship and medical debt.

Disparities in coverage and outcomes exacerbate the problem of healthcare accessibility. While some Americans enjoy comprehensive health insurance coverage through employer-sponsored plans or government programs like Medicare and Medicaid, millions remain uninsured or underinsured, lacking access to essential healthcare services. These disparities disproportionately affect marginalized communities, including low-income individuals, racial and ethnic minorities, and rural populations, exacerbating existing health inequalities.

Moreover, even among those with health insurance coverage, disparities in healthcare outcomes persist. Racial and ethnic minorities, in particular, experience higher rates of chronic diseases, lower life expectancy, and poorer health outcomes compared to their white counterparts. These disparities are driven by systemic factors such as structural racism, social determinants of health, and unequal access to quality healthcare services.

The deficiencies in the healthcare system undermine the fundamental principle of healthcare as a human right and call into question the nation's commitment to the welfare of its people. Affordable and quality healthcare promotes well-being, economic productivity, and social cohesion. When individuals cannot access necessary medical care, they are more likely to delay treatment, experience worsened health outcomes, and face financial hardship, ultimately undermining their quality of life and contributing to societal inequities.

Addressing the challenges of healthcare accessibility requires comprehensive reform that addresses the root causes of disparities and ensures that all Americans have access to affordable and quality healthcare services. This may involve expanding health insurance coverage, lowering prescription drug prices, investing in primary care and preventive services, and addressing social determinants of health such as poverty, housing, and food insecurity. By prioritizing healthcare accessibility, the United States can fulfill its obligation to ensure the well-being of all its citizens and build a healthier and more equitable society.

Healthcare Disparities

Disparities in healthcare access and outcomes persist along racial, ethnic, and socioeconomic lines in the United States, revealing deep-seated inequalities that undermine the nation's commitment to public health and well-being. Minority and marginalized communities often face barriers to healthcare that result in higher rates of preventable diseases, lower life expectancies, and diminished quality of life. These disparities highlight systemic flaws in the healthcare system and underscore the urgent need for equitable and inclusive healthcare policies and practices.

Unequal access to healthcare services is one of the most significant contributors to healthcare disparities. Minority and marginalized communities are more likely to experience barriers such as lack of health insurance coverage, limited access to healthcare facilities, transportation challenges, and language barriers. As a result, many individuals within these communities struggle to access preventive care, screenings, and timely medical treatments, leading to higher rates of undiagnosed or untreated health conditions.

Moreover, disparities in healthcare outcomes persist even among individuals with access to medical care. Racial and ethnic minorities, in particular, experience higher rates of chronic diseases such as diabetes, hypertension, heart disease, and certain cancers, as well as poorer health outcomes and lower life expectancies compared to their white counterparts. These disparities are often driven by a complex interplay of factors, including social determinants of health such as poverty, inadequate housing, food insecurity, and limited access to education and economic opportunities.

Healthcare disparities also reflect systemic biases and discrimination within the healthcare system itself. Studies have documented disparities in the quality of care provided to minority patients, including disparities in diagnosis, treatment, and pain management. Implicit biases among healthcare providers, lack of cultural competence, and unequal access to specialty care all contribute to disparities in healthcare outcomes and exacerbate existing health inequities.

The persistence of healthcare disparities underscores the need for comprehensive strategies to address the root causes of inequality and promote health equity for all Americans. This may involve implementing policies that expand access to affordable health insurance coverage, increasing funding for community health centers and safety-net hospitals serving underserved communities, improving cultural competency training for healthcare providers, and addressing social determinants of health through targeted interventions.

By prioritizing health equity and addressing healthcare disparities, the United States can fulfill its commitment to ensuring that all individuals, regardless of race, ethnicity, or socioeconomic status, have the opportunity to achieve optimal health and well-being. This requires a concerted effort from policymakers, healthcare providers, community organizations, and individuals alike to dismantle barriers to healthcare access and promote equitable healthcare delivery for all.

Handling The COVID-19 Pandemic

The handling of the COVID-19 pandemic has been a topic of intense debate and scrutiny, with various aspects of the response sparking contention and criticism. From public health measures to vaccine distribution and healthcare infrastructure, every facet of the pandemic response has faced scrutiny and evaluation.

One of the critical points of contention has been implementing and enforcing public health measures to control the spread of the virus. Measures such as mask mandates, social distancing guidelines, and lockdowns have been resisted by some population segments who view them as overly restrictive or infringing on personal freedoms. Debates have raged over the balance between protecting public health and preserving individual liberties, with differing opinions on the effectiveness and necessity of various measures.

Vaccine distribution has also been a contentious issue, with debates over prioritization, allocation, and access. Questions have been raised about the equity of vaccine distribution, particularly in marginalized communities that the virus has disproportionately impacted. Concerns over vaccine hesitancy, misinformation, and logistical challenges have complicated efforts to achieve widespread vaccination and herd immunity.

Furthermore, the pandemic has exposed vulnerabilities in the healthcare infrastructure, including shortages of critical supplies such as personal protective equipment (PPE) and ventilators, overwhelmed healthcare systems, and disparities in access to healthcare services. The strain on healthcare workers, who have been on the front lines of the pandemic response, has raised concerns about burnout, mental health, and workforce shortages.

Handling the COVID-19 pandemic has highlighted the importance of effective leadership, communication, and collaboration in responding to public health crises. It has underscored the need for evidence-based decision-making, transparent communication, and coordinated efforts across all levels of government and society. While there have been successes in controlling the spread of the virus and developing vaccines in record time, the pandemic has also exposed shortcomings and disparities that must be addressed to better prepare for future health emergencies.

Political Polarization

Political polarization in the United States has reached unprecedented levels, deepening divisions along partisan lines and hindering progress on crucial issues. The inability of lawmakers to find common ground and compromise has led to political gridlock, eroding confidence in the political system and undermining democratic principles.

At the heart of political polarization is the widening ideological gap between Democrats and Republicans, fueled by factors such as media echo chambers, gerrymandered districts, and the influence of special interest groups. This ideological divide has led to a breakdown in civil discourse and cooperation, with lawmakers more focused on scoring political points and appeasing their base than on finding solutions to pressing challenges.

The consequences of political polarization are far-reaching and profound. Gridlock in Congress has resulted in legislative stalemates and government shutdowns, preventing the passage of important legislation on issues such as healthcare, immigration reform, and climate change. As a result, critical problems remain unaddressed, exacerbating societal tensions and inequalities.

Furthermore, the perception of a dysfunctional government incapable of addressing the needs of its citizens has diminished America's standing on the world stage. International observers view the United States as increasingly divided and ineffective, raising doubts about its ability to lead on global issues and uphold democratic values. This erosion of soft power undermines America's influence and credibility in the international community.

Moreover, political polarization has fueled social unrest and division within American society, deepening distrust and hatred between political factions. Civility in political discourse has declined, with partisan rhetoric becoming increasingly hostile and divisive. This toxic political climate has contributed to a sense of alienation and disenchantment among many Americans, further eroding faith in democratic institutions.

Addressing political polarization requires a concerted effort from political leaders, civil society, and ordinary citizens alike. It requires bridging divides, fostering dialogue, and finding common ground on shared goals and values. By promoting civility, empathy, and respect for differing viewpoints, we can work towards a more inclusive and functional democracy that serves the needs of all citizens.

ADRIAN ROCQUECLIFFE

Gun Violence Epidemic

The United States grapples with a pervasive gun violence epidemic characterized by mass shootings and high rates of firearm-related deaths occurring with alarming frequency. This issue has profound implications for public safety and the well-being of communities nationwide. Yet, the failure to enact comprehensive gun control measures exacerbates the problem and contributes to a sense of insecurity among citizens.

Mass shootings, in particular, have become all too common in the United States, capturing headlines and sparking outrage each time they occur. These tragic events, which often target innocent civilians in places like schools, workplaces, and public spaces, leave lasting scars on communities and underscore the urgent need for action to address the root causes of gun violence.

Beyond mass shootings, firearm-related deaths occur at alarming rates in the United States, with homicides, suicides, and accidents claiming tens of thousands of lives each year. The easy accessibility of firearms, coupled with lax gun laws and loopholes in the background check system, contribute to the proliferation of guns and the perpetuation of violence.

The failure to enact comprehensive gun control measures exacerbates the problem of gun violence and undermines public safety. Despite widespread public support for measures such as universal background checks, restrictions on high-capacity magazines, and closing loopholes that allow individuals to purchase firearms without proper screening, progress on gun control legislation has been slow and incremental.

This failure to act is often attributed to political gridlock, special interest lobbying, and ideological divisions that have stymied efforts to pass meaningful gun reform at the federal level. The influence of the gun lobby, notably the National Rifle Association (NRA), has had a chilling effect on lawmakers, making it difficult to muster the political will necessary to enact meaningful change.

The consequences of inaction on gun violence are profound, undermining the right to safety and security for all citizens and perpetuating a cycle of fear and violence in communities across the country. Moreover, the failure to address the root causes of gun violence, including poverty, mental health issues, and systemic inequities, perpetuates social injustices and exacerbates disparities in access to safety and protection.

Addressing the gun violence epidemic requires a comprehensive approach that includes sensible gun control measures, investment in mental health services and community-based violence prevention programs, and addressing the underlying social determinants of violence. It also requires political leadership and courage to stand up to special interests and prioritize the safety and well-being of all Americans. By working together to enact evidence-based policies and initiatives, we can create safer communities and reduce the senseless loss of life caused by gun violence.

Criminal Justice System Issues

The United States grapples with a myriad of issues within its criminal justice system, contributing to one of the highest incarceration rates globally. This system disproportionately affects minority and low-income communities, leading to concerns about fairness, justice, and the effectiveness of punitive measures.

One of the most pressing issues is the disproportionate impact of the criminal justice system on minority communities, mainly Black and Hispanic individuals. Racial profiling by law enforcement, biased policing practices, and systemic racism within the criminal justice system result in higher rates of arrest, conviction, and harsher sentencing for individuals of color. This perpetuates cycles of inequality and undermines trust in law enforcement and the judicial system.

Harsh sentencing practices, including mandatory minimum sentences and three-strikes laws, contribute to the over-incarceration of individuals, particularly those convicted of nonviolent offenses. These punitive measures often result in lengthy prison sentences that do little to address underlying issues such as poverty, substance abuse, and mental illness. Instead, they exacerbate social inequalities and perpetuate cycles of incarceration and recidivism.

Inadequate rehabilitation programs and reentry support further compound the challenges faced by individuals involved in the criminal justice system. Limited access to education, job training, and mental health services within prisons and upon release hinder successful reintegration into society, increasing the likelihood of reoffending. This failure to address the root causes of criminal behavior undermines efforts to reduce recidivism and promote rehabilitation.

Moreover, the privatization of prisons and the profit motive in the criminal justice system have created perverse incentives that prioritize incarceration and profit over rehabilitation and public safety. Private prison companies lobby for policies that increase incarceration rates and oppose efforts to reform the system, perpetuating the cycle of mass incarceration and perpetuating social injustices.

Addressing these issues requires comprehensive reform prioritizing fairness, equity, and rehabilitation within the criminal justice system. This includes measures such as ending racial profiling, reforming sentencing laws to reduce reliance on incarceration, investing in diversion programs and community-based alternatives to incarceration, and providing comprehensive support services for individuals reentering society after incarceration. By addressing systemic inequalities and promoting restorative justice principles, we can create a more equitable and effective criminal justice system that serves the needs of all individuals and communities.

Income Inequality

Despite its status as a global economic powerhouse, the United States grapples with staggering levels of income inequality, which have profound implications for societal well-being and economic stability. The gap between the wealthy elite and the rest of the population continues to widen, leading to socioeconomic disparities and diminished opportunities for upward mobility.

This stark inequality challenges the notion of a fair and equitable society, tarnishing the image of American greatness.

At the heart of income inequality in the United States is the concentration of wealth among a small percentage of the population, often called the "one percent." This elite group controls a disproportionate share of the nation's wealth while most Americans struggle to make ends meet. This concentration of wealth exacerbates disparities in income, access to resources, and economic opportunities, perpetuating cycles of poverty and inequality.

One key driver of income inequality is the unequal distribution of income and wealth, which is influenced by factors such as globalization, technological advancements, and changes in labor markets. The decline of unions, stagnation of wages for low—and middle-income workers, and the rise of precarious employment contribute to widening income disparities and hinder efforts to achieve economic mobility.

Moreover, disparities in access to education, healthcare, and housing further exacerbate income inequality, creating barriers to social and economic advancement for disadvantaged communities. Structural factors such as systemic racism, discrimination, and unequal access to opportunities perpetuate inequalities and hinder efforts to promote upward mobility and equality of opportunity.

The consequences of income inequality are far-reaching and profound, affecting nearly every aspect of society. Socioeconomic disparities undermine social cohesion, exacerbate health inequalities, and contribute to social unrest and political polarization. Moreover, income inequality hinders economic growth and undermines the economy's stability, as a large wealth gap can lead to decreased consumer spending, reduced social mobility, and increased social tensions.

Addressing income inequality requires a multi-faceted approach that includes policies to promote equitable access to education, healthcare, and economic opportunities and measures to redistribute wealth and address systemic barriers to social and economic mobility. This may include raising the minimum wage, expanding access to affordable housing and healthcare, investing in education and workforce development programs, and implementing progressive tax policies to ensure the wealthy pay their fair share.

By addressing the root causes of income inequality and promoting policies that foster inclusive growth and opportunity for all Americans, the United States can work towards building a more equitable and prosperous society that reflects the values of fairness, justice, and American greatness.

Education System Challenges

The education system in the United States faces many challenges that contribute to disparities in resources and outcomes between schools in affluent and low-income communities. These challenges, including underfunding, overcrowded classrooms, and unequal access to educational opportunities, hinder the realization of every child's potential and undermine the nation's commitment to meritocracy and equal opportunity.

Underfunding is one of the most significant challenges facing the education system, particularly in schools serving low-income and minority students. These schools often lack sufficient resources for quality education, resulting in outdated textbooks, inadequate facilities, and limited extracurricular activities. The inequitable distribution of funding perpetuates disparities in educational outcomes and exacerbates social inequalities.

Overcrowded classrooms are another pressing issue, particularly in urban areas where population growth outpaces school infrastructure. Large class sizes make it difficult for teachers to provide individualized attention and support to students, leading to decreased academic performance and increased behavioral problems. Moreover, overcrowding strains resources and undermines the quality of education for all students, regardless of socioeconomic background.

Unequal access to educational opportunities further exacerbates disparities in educational outcomes. Students in low-income communities often lack access to advanced coursework, extracurricular activities, and enrichment programs available in more affluent schools. This perpetuates the cycle of poverty and limits opportunities for social and economic mobility, as students from disadvantaged backgrounds are less likely to receive the education and support they need to succeed.

Moreover, systemic factors such as racial segregation, discrimination, and cultural biases within the education system contribute to disparities in educational outcomes. Minority students, mainly Black and Hispanic students, are more likely to attend under-resourced schools, face harsher disciplinary practices, and experience lower graduation rates compared to their white counterparts. These inequities undermine the principles of fairness, justice, and equal opportunity upon which the education system is founded.

Addressing these challenges requires a concerted effort to prioritize equity and excellence in education. This may involve increasing funding for high-needs schools, reducing class sizes, expanding access to early childhood education and quality preschool programs, and implementing policies to promote diversity and inclusion within schools. Investing in every child's future and ensuring that all students have access to quality education can build a more equitable and prosperous society that reflects the values of meritocracy and equal opportunity.

Environmental Concerns

The United States faces pressing environmental concerns that threaten the planet's health and future generations' well-being. These issues, including climate change, pollution, and habitat destruction, require urgent action to mitigate their impacts and safeguard the environment for present and future generations. Despite being a significant contributor to global environmental degradation, the country has been criticized for its reluctance to adopt comprehensive measures to address these challenges, undermining its role as a global leader in environmental stewardship.

Climate change is one of the most pressing environmental challenges facing the United States and the world. Burning fossil fuels, deforestation, and industrial activities have steadily increased greenhouse gas emissions, resulting in rising global temperatures, melting polar ice caps, more frequent and severe weather events, and disruptions to ecosystems and biodiversity. Despite overwhelming scientific evidence of the human contribution to climate change and the urgent need for action, the United States has faced criticism for its slow response and lack of ambition in reducing emissions and transitioning to renewable energy sources.

Pollution is another significant environmental concern, with air, water, and soil pollution posing severe risks to human health and the environment. Industrial emissions, vehicle exhaust, agricultural runoff, and waste disposal contribute to pollution exceeding safe limits in many communities, particularly low-income and minority neighborhoods. The failure to regulate and mitigate pollution threatens public health, exacerbates environmental injustices, and undermines efforts to achieve sustainable development.

Habitat destruction and biodiversity loss are critical environmental issues driven by urbanization, industrial development, deforestation, and unsustainable land use practices. The loss of natural habitats and species extinction rates are accelerating at an alarming pace, leading to irreversible damage to ecosystems and their services, such as clean water, pollination, and climate regulation. The failure to prioritize conservation and sustainable land management jeopardizes biodiversity. It undermines ecosystems' resilience to withstand environmental stresses and disturbances.

The reluctance of the United States to adopt comprehensive measures to address environmental challenges is partly due to political and economic interests prioritizing short-term profits over long-term sustainability. The influence of fossil fuel industries, lobbying efforts, and political gridlock have hindered progress on environmental legislation and undermined efforts to transition to a low-carbon economy and sustainable development pathways.

Addressing environmental concerns requires a comprehensive approach integrating environmental protection, climate action, and sustainable development goals. This may involve policies to reduce greenhouse gas emissions, protect natural habitats, promote clean energy technologies, and strengthen environmental regulations and enforcement mechanisms. It also requires collective action and international cooperation to address global environmental challenges and build a more sustainable and resilient future for all. By prioritizing sustainability and conservation, the United States can fulfill its responsibility as a global environmental steward and protect the health and well-being of current and future generations.

International Relations

America's foreign policy decisions and interventions have been constantly scrutinized and debated, shaping the country's role and reputation on the global stage. From military interventions in distant lands to trade disputes with key allies, the actions of the United States have evoked both admiration and criticism, reflecting the complexity of international relations.

Military interventions have been a defining aspect of America's foreign policy, often drawing attention and controversy. While some interventions, - such as those aimed at combating terrorism or promoting democracy, have garnered support for their noble intentions, others have faced harsh criticism for their perceived imperialistic tendencies. Critics argue that interventions in sovereign nations without sufficient international support or legitimate cause can undermine global stability and fuel anti-American sentiment.

Trade disputes and negotiations have also been a prominent feature of America's engagement with the world. While the United States has championed free trade principles and played a leading role in shaping global trade policies, its approach to trade relations has sometimes sparked tension and conflict. Disputes over tariffs, intellectual property rights, and market access have strained relations with key trading partners and raised concerns about the future of international trade cooperation.

Criticism of America's foreign policy extends beyond specific actions to broader concerns about imperialism, unilateralism, and disregard for international norms. The perception of the United States as a hegemonic power that imposes its will on other nations without regard for their sovereignty or interests has fueled resentment and opposition. Moreover, the United States' unilateralist tendencies, characterized by its willingness to act alone and disregard multilateral institutions and agreements, have raised questions about its commitment to global cooperation and diplomacy.

Disregarding international norms and institutions has also been a contention in America's foreign policy. The international community has criticized and condemned the country's withdrawal from international agreements, such as the Paris Climate Accord and the Iran nuclear deal. Critics argue that America's reluctance to uphold its commitments to global cooperation and diplomacy undermines its credibility and leadership on the world stage.

In conclusion, America's foreign policy decisions and interventions have been a subject of intense scrutiny and controversy, reflecting the complex dynamics of international relations. While the United States plays a central role in shaping global affairs, criticisms of imperialism, unilateralism, and disregard for international norms challenge the perception of America as a beacon of freedom and democracy. As the country navigates its role in an increasingly interconnected world, it faces the challenge of balancing its strategic interests with its commitment to upholding global values and principles.

Issues Of Systemic Racism

Issues of systemic racism continue to plague societies around the world, including the United States, where incidents of police brutality and racial injustice have sparked outrage and fueled calls for comprehensive reforms. Systemic racism refers to the standardized practices, policies, and structures that perpetuate racial inequality and discrimination, often resulting in unequal treatment and outcomes for marginalized communities.

One of the most visible manifestations of systemic racism in the United States is police brutality, particularly towards Black and minority communities. The deaths of George Floyd, Breonna Taylor, and countless others at the hands of law enforcement have laid bare the pervasive nature of police violence and the disproportionate impact it has on communities of color. These incidents have sparked widespread protests and demands for accountability, as well as calls to defund or reform police departments to address systemic issues such as racial bias, excessive use of force, and lack of accountability.

Beyond policing, systemic racism permeates various sectors of society, including education, healthcare, housing, and employment. Disparities in access to quality education, healthcare services, and economic opportunities persist along racial lines, perpetuating cycles of poverty and marginalization. Discriminatory practices such as redlining, racial profiling, and voter suppression further exacerbate inequalities and undermine the principles of fairness and equality.

Addressing systemic racism requires a multi-faceted approach that addresses its root causes and systemic barriers to racial equality. This may include reforms to criminal justice systems to promote accountability and transparency, investments in education and job training programs to address disparities in access to opportunities, and policies to address structural inequalities in housing, healthcare, and economic development.

Moreover, addressing systemic racism requires a commitment to dismantling racist ideologies and promoting racial equity and inclusion in all aspects of society. This may involve initiatives to promote diversity and representation in leadership positions, promote cultural competency and anti-racism training, and foster dialogue and understanding across racial and ethnic lines.

While addressing systemic racism is a complex and challenging endeavor, it is essential for building a more just and equitable society. By confronting the root causes of racial inequality and discrimination and working towards systemic reforms, the United States can move closer to realizing its ideals of liberty, justice, and equality for all.

Racial Injustice

America's history is indeed marked by a legacy of systemic racism and discrimination, which continue to shape social, economic, and political realities today. Racial injustice permeates various aspects of American life, casting a shadow over the nation's claim to greatness and challenging its commitment to justice and equality for all citizens.

One of the most glaring manifestations of racial injustice in contemporary America is police brutality against Black Americans. Incidents of excessive use of force, racial profiling, and fatal encounters with law enforcement have sparked outrage and protests across the country. The deaths of George Floyd, Breonna Taylor, and numerous others have laid bare the deep-rooted racism within policing and underscored the urgent need for reform.

Disparities in healthcare and education further exacerbate racial injustice, perpetuating cycles of inequality and limiting opportunities for communities of color. Black Americans are disproportionately affected by chronic health conditions, lack of access to quality healthcare, and unequal treatment within the healthcare system. Similarly, disparities in educational outcomes, school funding, and disciplinary practices perpetuate inequalities and hinder academic and economic advancement opportunities.

Mass incarceration also serves as a stark reminder of racial injustice in America, with Black Americans disproportionately represented in the criminal justice system. Racially biased policing, sentencing disparities, and systemic inequities within the legal system contribute to the overrepresentation of Black individuals in prisons and jails. The criminalization of poverty and addiction further compounds these injustices, perpetuating cycles of incarceration and disenfranchisement.

The failure to address these injustices undermines the country's claim to greatness, erodes trust in institutions, and perpetuates social unrest. True greatness entails justice and equality for all citizens, regardless of race or ethnicity. By confronting systemic racism, addressing disparities, and promoting racial equity and inclusion policies, the United States can move closer to realizing its ideals of liberty, justice, and equality for all. This requires a collective commitment to challenging biases, dismantling discriminatory systems, and fostering a society where every individual has the opportunity to thrive.

Immigration Policies

Immigration policies and practices in the United States have long been a subject of contentious debates, drawing criticism from both domestic and international observers. The country's approach to immigration, characterized by a complex and often contradictory set of laws and regulations, has raised concerns about human rights violations and compassion towards immigrants.

One of the most contentious issues in recent years has been the policy of family separation, which resulted in the forced separation of thousands of migrant children from their parents at the U.S.-Mexico border. This practice, implemented as part of the Trump administration's "zero tolerance" policy towards illegal immigration, sparked widespread outrage and condemnation from human rights organizations, lawmakers, and the international community. Critics argue that family separation constitutes a grave violation of human rights and undermines the United States' moral authority on the global stage.

The detention of asylum seekers, particularly in overcrowded and inhumane conditions, has also drawn criticism for its impact on the health and well-being of migrants. The prolonged detention of individuals, including children and families, without adequate access to legal representation or due process raises concerns about the violation of international refugee law and the rights of asylum seekers. Moreover, the use of detention as a deterrent to migration undermines the United States' commitment to upholding human rights and protecting vulnerable populations.

Another major criticism of U.S. immigration policies is the lack of a comprehensive pathway to citizenship for undocumented immigrants living in the country. The estimated 11 million undocumented immigrants in the United States face numerous barriers to legal status and citizenship, including lengthy waiting periods, bureaucratic hurdles, and punitive measures such as deportation. The absence of a clear and accessible pathway to citizenship perpetuates insecurity and vulnerability among immigrant communities. It undermines efforts to promote integration and social cohesion.

In response to these criticisms, advocates for immigration reform have called for a more compassionate and humane approach to immigration policy. This includes reforms to end family separation, reform the asylum system to ensure fair and timely processing of claims, and create a pathway to citizenship for undocumented immigrants who meet specific criteria, such as paying taxes and passing background checks. Additionally, there have been calls to address the root causes of migration, such as poverty, violence, and political instability in sending countries, through foreign aid, diplomacy, and cooperation with international partners.

Ultimately, the debate over immigration policy in the United States reflects broader questions about national identity, security, and values. While there are legitimate concerns about border security and the rule of law, there is also a recognition of the need for compassion, fairness, and respect for human rights in the treatment of immigrants and asylum seekers. Finding a balance between these competing interests will require political leadership, public engagement, and a commitment to upholding the principles of justice, compassion, and dignity for all individuals, regardless of their immigration status.

Media Polarization And Misinformation

Media polarization and the spread of misinformation have emerged as significant challenges in contemporary society, exacerbating societal divisions and undermining trust in the media as a source of objective information. The proliferation of partisan media outlets and the rise of social media platforms has created echo chambers where individuals are exposed primarily to information that aligns with their pre-existing beliefs and biases.

One key consequence of media polarization is the erosion of trust in traditional media sources. Partisan media outlets, which cater to specific ideological viewpoints, often prioritize sensationalism and sensationalist reporting over factual accuracy, leading to a decline in credibility among the general public. Moreover, the spread of misinformation, deliberate falsehoods, and conspiracy theories further undermines the integrity of the media landscape, making it difficult for audiences to discern fact from fiction.

The echo chambers created by media polarization contribute to the fragmentation of society, hindering constructive dialogue and critical thinking. Individuals are increasingly isolated within their ideological bubbles, where dissenting viewpoints are dismissed or ignored, and alternative perspectives are rarely considered. This reinforces existing biases and prejudices, making engaging in meaningful discussions or finding common ground on important issues difficult.

Furthermore, media polarization and misinformation significantly challenge democratic governance and civic engagement. In an environment where truth is subjective and facts are malleable, it becomes increasingly difficult for citizens to make informed decisions and hold elected officials accountable. Political discourse devolves into partisan bickering and ideological warfare, making it challenging to address pressing issues and find solutions that benefit the common good.

Addressing media polarization and misinformation requires a multifaceted approach that involves media literacy education, regulatory reforms, and efforts to promote transparency and accountability in journalism. Educating the public about the dangers of misinformation and teaching critical thinking skills can empower individuals to navigate the media landscape more effectively and discern credible sources of information from unreliable ones. Additionally, regulatory measures to combat disinformation and promote transparency in media ownership and funding can help mitigate the spread of false information and hold media organizations accountable for their reporting practices.

Ultimately, overcoming media polarization and misinformation requires a collective effort from media organizations, policymakers, and civil society to promote a culture of truth, accuracy, and accountability in the media. By fostering a more informed and engaged citizenry, we can strengthen democracy, promote social cohesion, and build a more resilient society better equipped to address the complex challenges of the 21st century.

Infrastructure Deficiencies

Infrastructure deficiencies represent a pressing challenge for the United States, with aging bridges, roads, and public transportation systems in dire need of repair and modernization. Decades of underinvestment and deferred maintenance have taken their toll, resulting in deteriorating infrastructure that hinders economic growth and poses risks to public safety.

One of the country's most visible infrastructure challenges is its aging transportation networks. Many roads and bridges across the United States are well past their intended lifespan, with deteriorating conditions that pose safety risks to motorists and pedestrians alike. Crumbling infrastructure increases the likelihood of accidents and fatalities. Delays, congestion, and vehicle maintenance expenses significantly cost businesses and commuters.

Public transportation systems also suffer from chronic underinvestment and neglect, exacerbating congestion and pollution in urban areas and limiting access to jobs, education, and essential services for many Americans. Outdated and inadequate public transit infrastructure not only contributes to traffic congestion and air pollution but also exacerbates social and economic inequalities by limiting mobility options for low-income and marginalized communities.

Water and wastewater systems represent another critical area of infrastructure deficiency in the United States. Many cities and towns rely on aging pipes and treatment facilities susceptible to leaks, contamination, and system failures. Limiting access to clean water and sanitation services jeopardizes public health and undermines economic competitiveness and environmental sustainability.

Addressing infrastructure deficiencies requires significant investment and concerted efforts from federal, state, and local governments and private sector stakeholders. Infrastructure investment creates jobs, stimulates economic growth, improves productivity, enhances public safety, and strengthens communities' resilience to natural disasters and other emergencies.

Furthermore, investments in infrastructure should prioritize sustainability and resilience, incorporating climate adaptation measures and green technologies to mitigate the impacts of climate change and reduce greenhouse gas emissions. This includes upgrading transportation systems to support electric vehicles and expanding renewable energy sources to power infrastructure networks.

In conclusion, infrastructure deficiencies represent a significant challenge for the United States. Aging and deteriorating infrastructure threaten public safety, economic competitiveness, and environmental sustainability. Addressing these challenges requires bold action and sustained investment in modernizing and upgrading the country's transportation, water, energy, and communications systems. The United States can build a more prosperous, equitable, and resilient future for all Americans by prioritizing infrastructure investment and adopting sustainable and resilient solutions.

Student Debt Crisis

The student debt crisis in the United States has reached alarming levels, with rising tuition costs and mounting student loan debt burdening millions of Americans and limiting their financial freedom and economic mobility. This crisis has far-reaching implications, exacerbating income inequality and stifling opportunities for young people to pursue higher education and achieve their full potential.

One of the primary drivers of the student debt crisis is the skyrocketing cost of higher education. Over the past few decades, tuition and fees at colleges and universities have outpaced inflation, leaving many students and their families struggling to afford the cost of attendance. As a result, students increasingly rely on student loans to finance their education, leading to unprecedented student loan debt.

The burden of student loan debt disproportionately affects low- and middle-income families, exacerbating income inequality and widening the wealth gap. High levels of student debt can prevent individuals from achieving key milestones such as buying a home, starting a family, or saving for retirement, further perpetuating economic disparities and hindering social mobility.

Moreover, the student debt crisis has broader implications for the economy. Mounting levels of student debt can dampen consumer spending and hinder economic growth, as individuals are forced to divert a significant portion of their income towards loan payments rather than investing in goods, services, or savings. Additionally, high levels of student debt can deter young people from pursuing careers in public service, education, or other low-paying but socially valuable fields, exacerbating workforce shortages and undermining societal well-being.

Addressing the student debt crisis requires comprehensive reforms that address the root causes of rising tuition costs and unsustainable levels of student loan debt. This may include increasing public investment in higher education to reduce reliance on tuition revenue, implementing policies to make college more affordable and accessible, such as free community college or debt-free college programs, and providing relief for borrowers through loan forgiveness or refinancing initiatives.

Furthermore, financial literacy and education are needed to help students make informed decisions about borrowing and managing their finances. This includes providing resources and support for students to navigate the complex financial aid process, understand their loan options, and make responsible choices about borrowing and repayment.

Ultimately, addressing the student debt crisis is not only a matter of economic policy but also a moral imperative. By relieving the burden of student debt and making higher education more affordable and accessible for all Americans, we can create a more equitable and prosperous society where everyone can pursue their dreams and achieve their full potential.

Corporate Influence In Politics

Corporate influence in politics represents a significant challenge to democratic principles and the integrity of the political process. The undue influence of corporate interests on policymaking undermines the fundamental tenets of democracy and erodes public trust in government institutions.

One primary mechanism through which corporations exert influence in politics is lobbying. Corporations and special interest groups spend billions of dollars yearly lobbying to shape legislation and regulations to benefit their interests. This often involves hiring well-connected lobbyists, making campaign contributions to politicians, and funding political action committees (PACs) to influence elections and policy outcomes.

Campaign finance loopholes also contribute to corporate influence in politics. The proliferation of super PACs, dark money groups, and other forms of independent political spending allows corporations and wealthy individuals to funnel unlimited money into political campaigns, often without disclosing their donors. This flood of money can drown out the voices of ordinary citizens and give undue influence to wealthy donors and special interests.

Regulatory capture is another phenomenon that allows corporations to wield undue influence over the regulatory process. Regulatory agencies tasked with overseeing industries often become captured by the entities they are supposed to regulate, leading to lax regulation enforcement and industry-friendly policies. This revolving door between government and industry can result in regulatory decisions prioritizing corporate profits over public health, safety, and environmental protection.

The influence of corporate interests in politics raises severe concerns about the fairness and integrity of governance. Policymakers beholden to corporate donors and lobbyists may prioritize corporations' interests over the general public's needs. This can result in policies that benefit the wealthy and powerful at the expense of working families, exacerbating income inequality and perpetuating systemic injustices.

Moreover, corporate influence in politics can undermine public trust in government institutions and erode confidence in the democratic process. When citizens perceive that their elected officials are more responsive to corporate interests than to the needs and concerns of ordinary voters, it can lead to disillusionment and apathy, undermining the legitimacy of the political system.

Addressing corporate influence in politics requires comprehensive reforms to strengthen transparency, accountability, and government ethics. These may include measures to limit money's influence in politics, such as campaign finance reform, increased disclosure requirements for political spending, and restrictions on the revolving door between government and industry. Additionally, greater public awareness and engagement are needed to hold elected officials accountable and demand policies that serve the common good rather than narrow corporate interests.

Ultimately, safeguarding democracy requires ensuring that government remains responsive to the needs and interests of all citizens, not just the wealthy and powerful. By reducing the influence of corporate interests in politics, we can help restore faith in democratic institutions and build a more equitable and just society for all.

Erosion Of Civil Liberties

The erosion of civil liberties and privacy rights in the United States, especially in the aftermath of the 9/11 terrorist attacks, has sparked significant criticism and raised concerns about government overreach and the erosion of constitutional rights. Measures enacted in the name of national security, such as surveillance programs, warrantless wiretapping, and the expansion of executive powers, have been particularly contentious.

One of the most controversial responses to the 9/11 attacks was the passage of the USA PATRIOT Act, which granted broad surveillance powers to law enforcement and intelligence agencies. Under the PATRIOT Act, the government was authorized to conduct warrantless searches, monitor communications, and obtain personal records without judicial oversight, raising concerns about privacy and civil liberties violations.

In addition to legislative measures like the PATRIOT Act, the government has implemented extensive surveillance programs to monitor domestic and international communications. The National Security Agency (NSA), for example, has been involved in mass surveillance programs that collect metadata from phone calls and internet communications, leading to concerns about indiscriminate data collection and the infringement of privacy rights.

Warrantless wiretapping, conducted under the guise of national security, has further raised concerns about violations of due process and the Fourth Amendment protections against unreasonable searches and seizures. The government's use of secret surveillance courts and classified legal justifications has limited transparency and accountability, making it difficult for the public to assess the legality and scope of government surveillance activities.

The expansion of executive powers, particularly in national security and counterterrorism, has also raised alarm bells among civil liberties advocates. Executive actions such as targeted killings of suspected terrorists, indefinite detention without trial, and the use of secret military tribunals have raised questions about the balance of power between the executive, legislative, and judicial branches of government, as well as the protection of fundamental rights under the Constitution.

The erosion of civil liberties and privacy rights in the United States has significant implications for democracy, the rule of law, and individual freedoms. By sacrificing civil liberties in the name of national security, the government risks undermining the principles it seeks to protect and eroding public trust in democratic institutions. Moreover, the erosion of privacy rights can have chilling effects on free speech, political dissent, and the exercise of other fundamental rights essential to a free and democratic society.

Addressing the erosion of civil liberties requires a commitment to upholding constitutional principles, protecting privacy rights, and ensuring transparency and accountability in government. This may include reforms to surveillance laws, increased oversight of intelligence agencies, and judicial review of executive actions. Safeguarding civil liberties and privacy rights is essential for preserving democracy and upholding the values enshrined in the Constitution.

Systemic Corruption

Systemic corruption significantly threatens the political system's integrity and undermines public confidence in democratic governance. Instances of corruption and ethical lapses among elected officials and government institutions tarnish the reputation of public service and erode trust in the institutions entrusted with upholding the rule of law.

One of the most egregious forms of corruption is bribery, where public officials accept money or favors in exchange for political favors, government contracts, or favorable treatment. Bribery distorts the democratic process by allowing special interests to influence government decisions. It undermines the principle of equal representation and fairness in governance.

Embezzlement, another common form of corruption, involves misappropriating public funds or resources for personal gain. When government officials abuse their positions of power for financial gain, they not only deprive taxpayers of valuable resources but also undermine the effectiveness and legitimacy of government institutions.

Conflicts of interest also contribute to systemic corruption by creating opportunities for public officials to prioritize their personal or financial interests over the public good. When government officials have financial or personal ties to businesses or special interests that stand to benefit from their decisions, it raises questions about the integrity and impartiality of their actions.

The prevalence of corruption undermines the rule of law. It perpetuates a culture of impunity where corrupt behavior goes unchecked and unpunished. When corrupt officials are not held accountable for their actions, it conveys that corruption is acceptable and reinforces the belief that the political system is rigged in favor of the powerful and well-connected.

Moreover, corruption disproportionately affects marginalized and vulnerable populations by diverting resources from essential services such as healthcare, education, and infrastructure. When public funds are siphoned off through corruption, it exacerbates social and economic inequalities. It undermines efforts to address poverty and promote inclusive development.

Addressing systemic corruption requires a comprehensive approach that includes strengthening anti-corruption laws and enforcement mechanisms, promoting transparency and accountability in government, and fostering a culture of integrity and ethical leadership. This may include establishing independent anti-corruption agencies, implementing whistleblower protection laws, and improving transparency in government procurement processes.

Furthermore, promoting civic engagement and empowering citizens to hold their elected officials accountable is essential for combating corruption and safeguarding democratic governance.

Fostering a culture of transparency, accountability, and integrity in government can build public trust and confidence in democratic institutions and ensure that they serve the interests of all citizens, not just the privileged few.

Social Welfare Disparities

Social welfare disparities represent a significant challenge to addressing poverty and promoting socioeconomic equality in society. Disparities in access to social welfare programs, such as affordable housing, childcare, and food assistance, perpetuate cycles of poverty and exacerbate inequalities among different socioeconomic groups.

One key factor contributing to social welfare disparities is the inadequacy of social safety nets. Many social welfare programs are underfunded, understaffed, or poorly designed, leaving vulnerable populations without essential support systems to meet their basic needs. As a result, individuals and families facing economic hardship - often struggle to access vital resources and services that could help them overcome financial challenges and improve their quality of life.

Access to affordable housing is a critical issue that disproportionately affects low-income and marginalized communities. The lack of affordable housing options and the prevalence of housing discrimination can force individuals and families into unstable or unsafe living conditions, exacerbating homelessness and housing insecurity. Without stable housing, individuals and families may struggle to maintain employment, access healthcare, or pursue educational opportunities, further perpetuating cycles of poverty and social exclusion.

Similarly, access to affordable childcare is essential for working parents, particularly those with low incomes or single-parent households. However, high childcare costs and limited availability of affordable childcare options can create barriers to workforce participation and economic mobility, particularly for women and caregivers. Without access to quality childcare, parents may be forced to make difficult choices between work and caregiving responsibilities, hindering their ability to pursue education or career advancement opportunities.

Food insecurity is another significant issue affecting millions of individuals and families nationwide. Despite the existence of food assistance programs such as the Supplemental Nutrition Assistance Program (SNAP), many people still struggle to access an adequate and nutritious diet due to barriers such as stigma, eligibility requirements, and limited availability of healthy food options in underserved communities. Food insecurity not only has immediate health consequences but also perpetuates cycles of poverty and undermines long-term health and well-being.

Addressing social welfare disparities requires a multifaceted approach, including policy interventions and systemic changes to address the root causes of poverty and inequality. This may include increasing funding for social welfare programs, expanding access to affordable housing and childcare, and implementing policies that promote economic opportunity and social mobility for all individuals and families.

Additionally, efforts to combat social welfare disparities should prioritize the voices and experiences of marginalized communities and involve them in the design and implementation of solutions.

By centering the needs and perspectives of those most affected by social welfare disparities, policymakers can develop more effective and equitable policies that address the underlying structural barriers to socioeconomic equality and create a more just and inclusive society for all.

Decline In Global Standing

The decline in the United States' global standing represents a significant shift in the geopolitical landscape, characterized by diminishing influence and increasing challenges to its traditional leadership role on the world stage. Several factors have contributed to this decline, including concerns about isolationism, unilateralism, and the erosion of multilateral institutions.

One key factor contributing to the decline in global standing is the perception of isolationism in U.S. foreign policy. The United States' withdrawal from international agreements and organizations, such as the Paris Climate Agreement and the Iran nuclear deal, has raised concerns about its commitment to global cooperation and collective action. This retreat from international engagement has led to a perception of the United States as less reliable and less willing to assume its responsibilities as a global leader.

Unilateralism, or the tendency to act independently of international norms and institutions, has also undermined America's global standing. The use of military force without sufficient consultation or authorization from international bodies, as seen in conflicts such as the Iraq War, has strained relations with key allies and fueled resentment among other nations. This unilateral approach to foreign policy has eroded trust in U.S. leadership and weakened the country's ability to build consensus and coalitions to address global challenges.

Furthermore, the erosion of multilateral institutions and norms has undermined the United States' ability to address global challenges effectively. The Trump administration's skepticism towards international institutions such as the United Nations and the World Trade Organization, coupled with its attacks on multilateralism and globalization, has weakened international cooperation and diplomacy mechanisms. This has left a void in global governance that other countries, such as China, have sought to fill, further diminishing America's influence on the world stage.

The decline in U.S. global standing has significant implications for international affairs and the pursuit of global stability and prosperity. As the world's largest economy and military power, the United States has historically played a central role in shaping global norms, institutions, and alliances. However, its diminished influence has created opportunities for other countries to assert themselves on the world stage, leading to increased competition and uncertainty in international relations.

Addressing the decline in global standing requires a renewed commitment to international engagement, cooperation, and leadership. This may involve rejoining international agreements and organizations, strengthening alliances and partnerships, and promoting multilateral approaches to global challenges such as climate change, terrorism, and pandemics.

By reaffirming its commitment to global cooperation and leadership, the United States can regain its standing as a trusted and respected partner in the international community and help shape a more stable and prosperous world for future generations.

Erosion Of Trust In Institutions

The erosion of trust in institutions, spanning government, media, and the justice system, represents a profound challenge to society's fabric. In recent years, scandals, misinformation, and perceived biases have contributed to a significant decline in public confidence in the integrity and impartiality of critical societal institutions, undermining their ability to fulfill their roles effectively.

One of the primary factors contributing to the erosion of trust in institutions is the prevalence of scandals and corruption. Instances of misconduct or unethical behavior by government officials, corporate leaders, and other authority figures erode public confidence in the ability of institutions to act in the public interest. Whether political corruption, corporate fraud, or institutional cover-ups, each scandal further erodes trust and reinforces the perception of systemic rot within institutions.

Misinformation and spreading false or misleading information have also significantly undermined trust in institutions, particularly the media. The rise of social media and digital platforms has facilitated the rapid spread of misinformation, conspiracy theories, and partisan propaganda, making it difficult for the public to discern fact from fiction. This erosion of trust in the media undermines its role as a watchdog and a source of accurate information, further fueling skepticism and cynicism toward institutional authority.

Perceived biases and lack of transparency in institutions, including the justice system, further contribute to the erosion of trust. When individuals perceive that institutions are influenced by political agendas, corporate interests, or systemic biases, it undermines confidence in their ability to administer justice impartially and fairly. This perception of bias can lead to feelings of injustice and disenfranchisement, particularly among marginalized communities who may already face systemic discrimination within the justice system.

The erosion of trust in institutions has significant implications for democracy, governance, and social cohesion. When individuals lose faith in the institutions supposed to represent and serve them, it can lead to disengagement from civic life, political polarization, and a breakdown of social trust. This erosion of trust undermines the effectiveness of institutions. It hinders their ability to address pressing challenges such as inequality, corruption, and social injustice.

Rebuilding trust in institutions requires concerted efforts to promote transparency, accountability, and integrity in governance and leadership. This may include strengthening ethical standards, increasing transparency in decision-making processes, and fostering a culture of openness and responsiveness to public concerns. Additionally, rebuilding trust requires addressing underlying systemic issues such as inequality, discrimination, and political polarization, which can fuel distrust and undermine institutional legitimacy.

By rebuilding trust in institutions, we can strengthen democracy, promote social cohesion, and ensure that institutions serve the interests of all society members.

ADRIAN ROCQUECLIFFE

Access To Affordable Housing

Access to affordable housing is a pressing issue in the United States, where many individuals and families struggle to find safe and affordable places to live. The nation faces a housing affordability crisis driven by various factors, including rising rents, stagnant wages, and inadequate housing assistance programs. This crisis has far-reaching implications, contributing to homelessness, housing insecurity, and socioeconomic inequality while undermining the nation's commitment to providing opportunity and stability for all.

One of the primary drivers of the housing affordability crisis is the mismatch between rising housing costs and stagnant wages. In many parts of the country, rents and home prices have outpaced income growth, making it increasingly difficult for low- and moderate-income households to afford housing. As a result, many individuals and families are forced to spend a disproportionate amount of their income on housing, leaving them with less money for other essential needs such as healthcare, education, and food.

Another contributing factor to the housing affordability crisis is the inadequate supply of affordable housing. Many communities face shortages of affordable rental units and affordable homes for sale, exacerbating competition and increasing prices. Additionally, the lack of investment in affordable housing development and preservation has led to the deterioration of existing housing stock, further limiting options for low-income households.

The problem is compounded by the inadequacy of housing assistance programs, which fail to meet the needs of all eligible households. Programs such as Section 8 vouchers and public housing have lengthy waiting lists, leaving many families without the assistance to afford housing. Moreover, funding for these programs has been insufficient to keep pace with growing demand, resulting in limited resources and assistance for those most in need.

The housing affordability crisis has significant social and economic consequences. Homelessness and housing insecurity have devastating effects on individuals and families, contributing to poor health outcomes, educational disparities, and economic instability. Moreover, the lack of affordable housing perpetuates cycles of poverty and inequality, making it difficult for individuals and families to escape poverty and achieve upward mobility.

Addressing the housing affordability crisis requires a multifaceted approach that includes both short-term interventions and long-term solutions. In the short term, increasing funding for housing assistance programs, expanding rental assistance vouchers, and implementing rent stabilization measures can help alleviate immediate housing needs and prevent homelessness. In the long term, investing in affordable housing development, preserving existing housing stock, and promoting inclusive zoning policies can help create more equitable and sustainable housing markets.

The United States can fulfill its commitment to providing opportunity and stability for all its residents by addressing the housing affordability crisis.

Veterans' Issues

Veterans' issues represent a significant challenge in the United States, as many veterans face difficulties reintegrating into civilian life after their military service. These challenges span various areas, including healthcare, employment, and housing, and highlight systemic failures to fulfill the nation's obligations to those who have served.

One of the most pressing veterans' issues is access to healthcare, particularly mental healthcare. Many veterans struggle with post-traumatic stress disorder (PTSD), depression, and other mental health conditions as a result of their military service. However, the Department of Veterans Affairs (VA) healthcare system often faces challenges in providing timely and comprehensive mental health services to veterans. Long wait times, limited access to specialized care, and stigma surrounding mental health issues can prevent veterans from seeking the help they need, exacerbating their suffering and increasing their risk of suicide.

In addition to mental healthcare, veterans may also face challenges accessing other healthcare services, including primary care, specialized medical treatment, and prescription medications. Delays in VA benefits processing and administrative hurdles can further complicate veterans' ability to access healthcare, leaving them without essential medical services and support.

Employment is another significant issue for veterans transitioning to civilian life. While many veterans possess valuable skills and experiences gained through military service, they may struggle to find employment opportunities that match their qualifications and meet their financial needs. Challenges such as translating military experience into civilian terms, addressing gaps in employment history due to military service, and navigating the job market can make it difficult for veterans to secure meaningful and sustainable employment.

Housing instability and homelessness are also prevalent among veterans, particularly those who face difficulties accessing healthcare and employment. Veterans experiencing homelessness - often lack access to stable housing, leaving them vulnerable to exploitation, abuse, and poor health outcomes. While efforts have been made to address veteran homelessness through programs such as the VA's Supportive Services for Veteran Families (SSVF) program and HUD-VASH (Veterans Affairs Supportive Housing) vouchers, challenges remain in providing comprehensive support and assistance to veterans in need.

Addressing veterans' issues requires a coordinated and comprehensive approach that involves government agencies, community organizations, and healthcare providers working together to provide support and services to veterans. This may include improving access to mental healthcare, streamlining VA benefits processing, expanding employment and training opportunities for veterans, and increasing access to affordable housing and supportive services.

By prioritizing the needs of veterans and addressing the systemic barriers they face, the nation can fulfill its obligation to those who have served and ensure they receive the care and support they deserve.

Disparities In Access To Justice

Disparities in access to justice represent a significant challenge in the United States, where marginalized communities often face barriers to legal representation and fair treatment in the legal system. These disparities undermine the principles of equality and fairness under the law and perpetuate systemic injustices that disproportionately affect vulnerable populations.

One of the critical issues contributing to disparities in access to justice is racial profiling and discriminatory practices within the criminal justice system. Studies have consistently shown that people of color, mainly Black and Hispanic individuals, are more likely to be targeted by law enforcement, arrested, and subjected to harsher treatment within the legal system compared to their white counterparts. Racial profiling and discriminatory policing practices not only undermine trust in law enforcement but also perpetuate systemic racism and inequality within the criminal justice system.

Discriminatory sentencing practices further exacerbate disparities in access to justice, with people of color often receiving harsher sentences than white defendants for similar offenses. Factors such as mandatory minimum sentences, racial bias among judges and prosecutors, and disparities in access to quality legal representation contribute to unequal outcomes in the legal system. These disparities not only result in unjust outcomes for individuals but also perpetuate cycles of poverty and incarceration within marginalized communities.

Lack of resources for indigent defendants is another significant barrier to access to justice, particularly for low-income individuals who cannot afford private legal representation. Public defenders, often overwhelmed with caseloads and underfunded, may lack the time and resources to effectively represent their clients, leading to unequal treatment and outcomes in the legal system. Additionally, legal aid services, which provide free or low-cost legal assistance to low-income individuals, often face funding shortages and limited capacity, further limiting access to justice for marginalized communities.

Addressing disparities in access to justice requires systemic reforms to promote equity, fairness, and accountability within the legal system. This may include implementing policies to address racial bias and discrimination in policing and sentencing, increasing funding for public defender offices and legal aid services, and expanding access to diversion and alternative sentencing programs.

Additionally, efforts to promote diversity and inclusion within the legal profession can help ensure that legal representation reflects the communities it serves and is better equipped to address the needs of marginalized populations.

By addressing disparities in access to justice, the United States can work towards a legal system that upholds the principles of equality and fairness for all individuals, regardless of race, ethnicity, income, or social status.

Food Insecurity

Food insecurity remains a pressing issue in the United States despite its status as one of the wealthiest nations globally. Millions of Americans struggle with inadequate access to nutritious and affordable food, highlighting systemic failures to address basic human needs and ensure food security for all citizens.

One of the primary drivers of food insecurity is poverty. Low-income households often lack the financial resources to purchase an adequate and nutritious diet, leading to reliance on cheap and unhealthy food options or skipping meals altogether. Poverty rates in the United States, particularly among children and minorities, have remained stubbornly high, exacerbating the problem of food insecurity and perpetuating cycles of hunger and poverty.

Unemployment and underemployment also contribute to food insecurity, as individuals and families may struggle to afford necessities, including food, during economic hardship. The loss of a job or reduced work hours can have devastating consequences for household finances, leading to increased reliance on food assistance programs and charitable food resources to meet basic needs.

Disparities in access to healthy food options further exacerbate food insecurity, particularly in low-income and marginalized communities. Many low-income neighborhoods lack grocery stores and other sources of fresh, healthy food, leading to reliance on convenience stores and fast food outlets that offer limited options for nutritious eating. This lack of access to healthy food options, known as food deserts, contributes to poor dietary habits, chronic health conditions, and higher rates of food insecurity within these communities.

Food insecurity significantly affects individuals' health and well-being, contributing to malnutrition, chronic diseases, and poor academic and economic outcomes. Children from food-insecure households are more likely to experience developmental delays, academic difficulties, and health problems compared to their food-secure counterparts. Additionally, food insecurity can perpetuate cycles of poverty and inequality, hindering individuals' ability to reach their full potential and participate fully in society.

Addressing food insecurity requires a multifaceted approach that includes both short-term interventions and long-term solutions. In the short term, expanding access to food assistance programs such as the Supplemental Nutrition Assistance Program (SNAP) and school meal programs can help alleviate immediate hunger and food insecurity. Investing in community-based initiatives such as food banks, food pantries, and community gardens can also help provide nutritious food to needy individuals and families.

In the long term, addressing the root causes of food insecurity, including poverty, unemployment, and disparities in access to healthy food options, requires comprehensive policies and programs to promote economic opportunity, reduce income inequality, and improve access to affordable, nutritious food for all Americans.

By addressing food insecurity, the United States can ensure that all individuals have the opportunity to lead healthy, productive lives and contribute to the well-being of their communities.

Disability Rights

Disability rights are a critical issue in the United States, as people with disabilities continue to face significant barriers to full participation in society. These barriers, which include discrimination, lack of accessibility, and limited opportunities for employment and education, undermine the nation's commitment to equality and inclusion for all citizens.

One of the most pervasive barriers faced by people with disabilities is discrimination, both in the workplace and in society at large. Despite legal protections provided by the Americans with Disabilities Act (ADA), many individuals with disabilities encounter prejudice and bias when seeking employment, housing, and access to public accommodations. Discrimination can manifest in various forms, including hiring practices that favor non-disabled candidates, inaccessible facilities and transportation systems, and negative stereotypes that perpetuate stigma and social exclusion.

Lack of accessibility is another significant challenge for people with disabilities, as many public spaces, buildings, and services remain inaccessible to individuals with mobility, sensory, or cognitive impairments. Despite legal requirements for accessibility under the ADA, many businesses, government agencies, and public institutions fail to provide adequate accommodations for people with disabilities, limiting their ability to participate in community life and access essential services fully.

Limited opportunities for employment and education further compound the challenges faced by people with disabilities. Many individuals with disabilities encounter barriers to accessing quality education and training programs that would enable them to pursue meaningful and sustainable employment opportunities. Moreover, discriminatory attitudes and practices within the workforce often result in lower employment rates, lower wages, and limited career advancement opportunities for people with disabilities, perpetuating cycles of poverty and exclusion.

Adequate accommodations, such as assistive technologies, reasonable workplace accommodations, and accessible transportation options, enable people with disabilities to participate fully in society and exercise their rights. However, many individuals with disabilities encounter barriers to accessing these accommodations, either due to a lack of awareness, financial constraints, or bureaucratic hurdles.

Stigma and social isolation further exacerbate the challenges faced by people with disabilities, as negative attitudes and misconceptions about disability can lead to social exclusion, loneliness, and diminished self-esteem. Addressing stigma and promoting greater awareness and understanding of disability issues is essential for fostering a more inclusive and supportive society where all individuals are valued and respected for their abilities and contributions.

Ensuring the full participation and inclusion of people with disabilities requires concerted efforts from government, businesses, communities, and individuals to remove barriers, promote accessibility, and combat discrimination.

By upholding the principles of equality, dignity, and respect for all individuals, the United States can fulfill its commitment to disability rights and create a society where everyone has the opportunity to thrive and contribute fully to their communities.

Lack Of Affordable Childcare

The lack of affordable childcare is a pressing issue in the United States. It significantly burdens working families and hinders economic mobility and gender equality. The high cost of childcare strains family budgets and limits workforce participation, particularly for women who often bear the primary responsibility for caregiving.

Childcare costs in the United States are among the highest in the world, with many families spending a significant portion of their income on childcare expenses. For low- and middle-income families, the cost of childcare can be prohibitive, often exceeding the cost of rent or mortgage payments. As a result, many families are forced to make difficult choices between paying for childcare, meeting other essential expenses, or forgoing employment opportunities altogether.

The lack of affordable childcare options also significantly affects workforce participation and economic mobility. Many parents, particularly mothers, cannot work or pursue higher education or training opportunities due to the high cost of childcare. This limits their ability to earn income and support their families and reduces their potential for career advancement and financial stability in the long term.

Moreover, the lack of affordable childcare perpetuates gender inequality in the workforce, as women are disproportionately affected by the burden of caregiving responsibilities. Women are more likely than men to reduce their hours, leave the workforce temporarily, or opt out of the labor market altogether to care for children, limiting their earning potential and career advancement opportunities. This contributes to the gender wage gap and perpetuates inequalities in economic opportunity and financial security.

Addressing the lack of affordable childcare requires a multifaceted approach, including policy solutions and community-based initiatives. Investing in high-quality, affordable childcare options, such as childcare subsidies, tax credits, and publicly funded preschool programs, can help alleviate the financial burden on working families and increase access to childcare for all children, regardless of income.

Additionally, promoting workplace policies that support work-life balance, such as paid family leave, flexible work arrangements, and on-site childcare facilities, can help parents manage their caregiving responsibilities while remaining engaged in the workforce. Community-based initiatives, such as childcare cooperatives, shared childcare arrangements, and community centers, can provide affordable childcare options and support networks for needy families.

By addressing the lack of affordable childcare, the United States can support working families, promote economic mobility, and advance gender equality in the workforce. Investing in accessible and affordable childcare is a matter of economic necessity and a fundamental step towards building a more equitable and inclusive society where all families can thrive.

Tuition Debt Crisis

The tuition debt crisis in the United States represents a significant barrier to economic mobility and financial independence for millions of college graduates. Rising tuition costs and the burden of student loan debt have created a financial burden that delays the achievement of key life milestones and limits opportunities for advancement and prosperity.

One of the primary drivers of the tuition debt crisis is the escalating cost of higher education. Over the past few decades, tuition rates at colleges and universities have risen dramatically, outpacing inflation and wage growth. As a result, many students and their families are forced to take out loans to cover the cost of tuition, fees, room, board, and other educational expenses.

The burden of student loan debt falls disproportionately on young people, who are often just beginning their careers and may not have established stable sources of income. High levels of student loan debt can delay financial independence, forcing graduates to postpone major life decisions such as buying a home, starting a family, or saving for retirement. Additionally, student loan payments can consume a significant portion of graduates' income, limiting their ability to invest in their future, build wealth, and achieve long-term financial security.

The student debt crisis also exacerbates generational inequalities, as younger generations struggle to repay loans while facing stagnant wages, rising living costs, and limited job opportunities. Many millennials and members of Generation Z are saddled with tens of thousands of dollars in student loan debt, making it difficult to achieve the same level of economic stability and success as previous generations.

Moreover, the student debt crisis has broader implications for the economy. High levels of student loan debt can depress consumer spending, reduce homeownership rates, and dampen entrepreneurship and innovation. Additionally, the burden of student loan debt can contribute to mental health issues, stress, and anxiety among borrowers, further impacting their overall well-being and quality of life.

Addressing the tuition debt crisis requires a comprehensive approach, including short-term relief measures and long-term structural reforms. Short-term solutions may include expanding loan forgiveness programs, reducing interest rates on student loans, and providing financial assistance to borrowers in financial distress. Long-term reforms may include making higher education more affordable and accessible, increasing funding for public colleges and universities, and implementing policies to reduce the reliance on student loans to finance education.

By addressing the tuition debt crisis, the United States can promote economic mobility, reduce generational inequalities, and ensure that higher education remains a pathway to opportunity and prosperity for all Americans. Investing in affordable education and reducing the burden of student loan debt is a matter of economic necessity and a moral imperative to ensure everyone can achieve their full potential and contribute to society.

Urban Decay And Blight

Urban decay and blight are pressing issues facing many cities in the United States, characterized by vacant properties, deteriorating infrastructure, and high crime levels. These challenges have profound implications for the quality of life of residents and the overall vitality of urban communities.

Several factors contribute to urban decay and blight, including disinvestment, economic inequality, and racial segregation. Many urban areas have historically experienced disinvestment as industries relocated, jobs moved to suburban areas, and populations declined. This disinvestment has led to the abandonment of properties, the deterioration of infrastructure, and a decline in property values.

Economic inequality exacerbates the challenges of urban decay and blight, as low-income neighborhoods often bear the brunt of disinvestment and neglect. Residents in these communities may lack access to quality education, healthcare, and employment opportunities, perpetuating cycles of poverty and disinvestment. Moreover, the concentration of poverty can contribute to social problems such as crime, substance abuse, and poor physical and mental health outcomes.

Racial segregation also plays a significant role in urban decay and blight, as historically marginalized communities, particularly those of color, are disproportionately affected by disinvestment and neglect. Decades of discriminatory housing policies, such as redlining and restrictive covenants, have concentrated poverty and limited opportunities for economic advancement in minority neighborhoods. These patterns of segregation have contributed to disparities in neighborhood conditions, with predominantly white neighborhoods often receiving more significant investment and resources than predominantly non-white neighborhoods.

The consequences of urban decay and blight are far-reaching, impacting residents' health, safety, and overall well-being. Vacant properties and abandoned lots can become magnets for crime, vandalism, and illegal dumping, creating blighted landscapes that erode community pride and cohesion. Deteriorating infrastructure, such as crumbling roads and outdated utilities, can harm public health and safety, exacerbating residents' dislocation and disenfranchisement.

Addressing urban decay and blight requires a comprehensive approach that addresses the root causes of these challenges and promotes equitable and inclusive development. This may include targeted investment in infrastructure and community revitalization efforts, such as affordable housing development, small business support, and neighborhood beautification projects. Additionally, policies aimed at combating economic inequality and racial segregation, such as equitable economic development strategies and fair housing initiatives, are essential for creating more vibrant, resilient, and inclusive urban communities.

By addressing urban decay and blight, cities can create healthier, safer, and more vibrant communities where all residents have the opportunity to thrive and prosper. Investing in urban revitalization is essential for improving the quality of life for current residents, attracting new investment, fostering economic growth, and ensuring the long-term viability and sustainability of urban areas.

Public Transportation Deficiencies

Public transportation deficiencies represent a significant challenge for many communities in the United States, contributing to congestion, pollution, and inequities in access to transportation options. Despite efforts to improve infrastructure and expand services, the country lags behind other developed nations in terms of public transportation accessibility and quality.

One of the primary factors contributing to public transportation deficiencies is inadequate funding. Many public transit systems across the United States operate on tight budgets, relying heavily on fare revenue and government subsidies to cover operating costs. Limited funding can result in service cuts, reduced frequency, and outdated infrastructure, making public transportation less reliable and attractive to potential riders.

Outdated systems also contribute to public transportation deficiencies in the United States. Many cities rely on aging infrastructure, including outdated buses, trains, and stations, which can lead to service disruptions, delays, and safety concerns. Moreover, the lack of investment in modernizing and expanding public transit systems limits the ability to meet growing demand and address changing mobility needs.

Limited coverage is another challenge facing public transportation in the United States. Many rural and low-income communities lack access to public transit options, forcing residents to rely on personal vehicles or expensive alternatives such as ride-hailing services or private shuttles. This lack of coverage exacerbates transportation inequities and limits mobility for individuals who cannot afford or access private transportation options.

Deficits in public transportation infrastructure and accessibility have far-reaching consequences for individuals and communities. Congestion and pollution from increased reliance on personal vehicles contribute to environmental degradation and public health concerns, particularly in urban areas. Moreover, transportation inequities can exacerbate socioeconomic disparities, limiting access to jobs, education, healthcare, and other essential services for marginalized populations.

Addressing public transportation deficiencies requires a multifaceted approach that includes increased funding, modernization of infrastructure, and expansion of services to underserved communities. Investing in public transit can yield numerous benefits, including reducing traffic congestion, improving air quality, and enhancing access to opportunities for all residents. Moreover, prioritizing public transportation can promote economic development, spur job creation, and enhance the overall quality of life in communities nationwide.

By prioritizing public transportation as a critical component of the nation's transportation infrastructure, the United States can build more sustainable, equitable, and resilient transportation systems that meet the needs of all residents. Investing in public transit is essential for addressing current transportation deficiencies and creating more vibrant, connected, and livable communities for future generations.

Affordable Childcare

Affordable childcare is a critical issue facing many working families in the United States. The high cost of childcare places a significant burden on parents, particularly women, who often bear the primary responsibility for caregiving. Limited access to affordable childcare options not only impedes workforce participation and economic mobility but also perpetuates gender inequality, highlighting systemic challenges in supporting working families.

The cost of childcare in the United States is among the highest in the world, with many families spending a substantial portion of their income on childcare expenses. For low- and middle-income families, the cost of childcare can exceed rent or mortgage payments, making it financially challenging for parents to afford quality care for their children while meeting other essential expenses.

The high cost of childcare has significant implications for workforce participation, particularly for women. Many parents, especially mothers, are forced to reduce their hours, take lower-paying jobs, or leave the workforce to care for their children, resulting in lost income and career advancement opportunities. This phenomenon, known as the "childcare penalty," not only limits women's earning potential but also perpetuates gender inequality in the workforce.

Moreover, limited access to affordable childcare exacerbates economic inequality and hinders upward mobility for low-income families. Without access to quality childcare, parents may struggle to maintain stable employment or pursue educational and training opportunities, further perpetuating cycles of poverty and economic disadvantage.

The lack of affordable childcare options has broader societal implications, including reduced productivity, lower workforce participation rates, and diminished economic growth. By hindering workforce participation and economic mobility, the high cost of childcare stifles innovation, entrepreneurship, and overall economic prosperity.

Addressing childcare affordability requires a multifaceted approach that includes policy solutions and community-based initiatives. Policymakers can play a critical role in expanding access to affordable childcare through initiatives such as subsidies, tax credits, and publicly funded preschool programs. Additionally, investing in childcare infrastructure and workforce development can help improve the quality and availability of childcare options for families nationwide.

Community-based initiatives, such as childcare cooperatives, shared childcare arrangements, and employer-sponsored childcare programs, can also play a significant role in addressing the affordability of childcare at the local level. By leveraging community resources and fostering collaboration among stakeholders, these initiatives can help reduce costs, expand access, and improve the quality of childcare for families in need.

Overall, ensuring access to affordable childcare is essential for supporting working families, promoting economic mobility, and advancing gender equality in the workforce. By investing in affordable childcare options, policymakers and communities can create more equitable and inclusive societies where all families have the opportunity to thrive and succeed.

Access To Mental Healthcare

Access to mental healthcare in the United States is hindered by a multitude of barriers, including high costs, stigma, and a shortage of providers. These challenges contribute to a significant gap between the need for mental health services and the availability of care, leaving many Americans without access to essential treatment and support.

One of the primary barriers to accessing mental healthcare is the high cost of services. Mental health treatment can be prohibitively expensive for many individuals, particularly those without adequate insurance coverage or financial resources. Even with insurance, copayments, deductibles, and out-of-pocket expenses can pose significant financial burdens, deterring individuals from seeking the care they need.

The stigma surrounding mental illness also presents a barrier to accessing mental healthcare. Despite efforts to raise awareness and reduce stigma, negative attitudes and misconceptions about mental health continue to persist in society. Fear of judgment, discrimination, and social isolation can prevent individuals from seeking help for mental health concerns, leading to delayed or untreated illness and exacerbating symptoms over time.

Furthermore, the shortage of mental health providers exacerbates the challenges of accessing care. Many areas, mainly rural and underserved communities, lack an adequate number of mental health professionals, including psychiatrists, psychologists, therapists, and counselors. Long wait times for appointments and limited availability of services can further impede access to care, particularly for individuals in crisis or in need of urgent intervention.

The consequences of limited access to mental healthcare are far-reaching, impacting individuals, families, and communities. Untreated mental illness can lead to significant personal suffering, impaired functioning, and diminished quality of life. It can also contribute to other health problems, including substance abuse, chronic medical conditions, and increased risk of suicide.

Addressing barriers to mental healthcare requires a comprehensive approach that includes policy solutions and community-based initiatives. Policymakers can play a critical role in expanding access to mental health services through increased funding for mental health programs, integrating mental health services into primary care settings, and implementing telehealth services to reach underserved populations.

Community-based initiatives, such as mental health education and outreach programs, peer support groups, and crisis intervention services, can also help reduce stigma and increase awareness of available resources. By fostering collaboration among stakeholders and leveraging community resources, these initiatives can help connect individuals to the care and support they need to manage their mental health effectively.

Ensuring access to mental healthcare is essential for promoting overall health and well-being, reducing stigma, and building more resilient and supportive communities.

By addressing barriers to care and expanding access to services, policymakers and communities can help ensure that all individuals have the opportunity to live healthy, fulfilling lives.

Veterans' Healthcare Challenges

Veterans' healthcare challenges within the Department of Veterans Affairs (VA) system are multifaceted and have significant implications for the well-being of those who have served in the military. Despite efforts to improve veterans' access to healthcare services, several persistent issues hinder timely and high-quality care.

One of the primary challenges facing veterans is long wait times for appointments and treatments within the VA healthcare system. Delays in scheduling appointments can result in prolonged suffering for veterans in need of medical attention, exacerbating their health conditions and diminishing their quality of life. Furthermore, long wait times may contribute to feelings of frustration and disillusionment among veterans, eroding trust in the VA healthcare system.

Bureaucratic red tape is another significant barrier to veterans' access to healthcare services. The VA's complex administrative processes and paperwork requirements can create obstacles for veterans seeking care, leading to delays in receiving services and navigating the system. Additionally, bureaucratic inefficiencies may result in missed opportunities for early intervention and treatment, further compromising veterans' health outcomes.

Limited access to specialized care is a common challenge for veterans within the VA healthcare system. While the VA offers a wide range of medical services, including primary care, mental health, and rehabilitation, some areas may have limited access to specialized care, such as orthopedics, neurology, and oncology. Veterans requiring specialized treatments may face extended wait times or travel long distances to access care, posing logistical and financial burdens.

Disparities in veterans' health outcomes are a concerning consequence of these challenges within the VA healthcare system. Veterans from marginalized or underserved populations, such as racial and ethnic minorities, women, and LGBTQ+ individuals, may experience additional barriers to accessing care and may be at increased risk of experiencing poor health outcomes as a result. Addressing these disparities requires targeted efforts to improve access to culturally competent and inclusive healthcare services for all veterans.

Addressing veterans' healthcare challenges requires a multifaceted approach, including systemic reforms and targeted interventions. Streamlining administrative processes, reducing bureaucratic barriers, and improving efficiency within the VA healthcare system can help alleviate wait times and improve access to care for veterans. Additionally, expanding partnerships with community healthcare providers and increasing access to telehealth services can help bridge gaps in specialized care and enhance veterans' access to timely and high-quality services.

Furthermore, investing in workforce development and training programs for VA healthcare providers can help ensure veterans receive culturally competent and inclusive care that meets their unique needs.

By addressing these challenges and enhancing veterans' access to healthcare services, policymakers and stakeholders can honor their commitment to supporting those who have served our country and safeguarding their health and well-being.

Inequities In Educational Opportunities

Inequities in educational opportunities remain a persistent challenge in the United States, perpetuating systemic barriers to academic success for students from low-income and minority backgrounds. These disparities, rooted in historical and structural inequalities, contribute to a cycle of educational disadvantage that disproportionately affects marginalized communities.

One of the primary factors contributing to inequities in educational opportunities is the underfunding of schools serving low-income and minority students. Many schools in disadvantaged communities lack adequate resources, including qualified teachers, updated instructional materials, and modern facilities. As a result, students in these schools may not receive the same quality of education as their peers in more affluent areas, limiting their academic achievement and future opportunities.

Unequal access to resources further exacerbates disparities in educational opportunities. Students from low-income and minority backgrounds may lack access to essential educational resources, such as textbooks, technology, and extracurricular activities, which are critical for academic success. Moreover, disparities in access to advanced coursework, such as Advanced Placement (AP) classes and gifted programs, can perpetuate inequalities in academic achievement and college readiness.

Disciplinary practices within schools also contribute to inequities in educational opportunities. Students from low-income and minority backgrounds are more likely to experience harsh disciplinary measures, such as suspension and expulsion, compared to their peers. These punitive measures not only disrupt students' education but also contribute to the school-to-prison pipeline, perpetuating cycles of incarceration and further marginalizing already disadvantaged communities.

Furthermore, systemic biases and stereotypes can influence educators' expectations and perceptions of students from low-income and minority backgrounds, contributing to lower academic outcomes and limited opportunities for advancement. These biases may result in tracking and placement decisions that disproportionately affect marginalized students, limiting their access to rigorous coursework and opportunities for academic enrichment.

Addressing inequities in educational opportunities requires a comprehensive approach that includes policy reforms and targeted interventions. Increasing funding for schools serving low-income and minority students, implementing equitable resource allocation policies, and investing in strategies to recruit and retain diverse and culturally responsive educators can help level the playing field and improve student outcomes.

Additionally, promoting inclusive and culturally relevant curricula, implementing restorative justice practices, and providing comprehensive support services can help create a more supportive and nurturing learning environment for students from marginalized backgrounds.

By addressing the root causes of educational inequities and fostering a culture of equity and inclusion within schools, policymakers and educators can work towards ensuring that all students have access to the resources, opportunities, and support they need to thrive academically and beyond.

Limited Access To Affordable Higher Education

Limited access to affordable higher education in the United States poses significant barriers to individuals seeking to pursue their academic aspirations and undermines the principle of meritocracy. The rising cost of higher education has fueled a student debt crisis, burdening many students and graduates with substantial loan debt and hindering their social mobility.

One of the primary factors contributing to limited access to affordable higher education is the skyrocketing tuition and fees at colleges and universities across the country. Over the past few decades, the cost of attending college has far outpaced inflation, making higher education increasingly unaffordable for many students and their families. As a result, students from low-income and middle-income backgrounds may be forced to take on significant debt to finance their education or forgo higher education altogether.

The student debt crisis exacerbates economic inequality and perpetuates cycles of poverty by burdening individuals with financial obligations that can take decades to repay. High levels of student loan debt can limit graduates' ability to pursue careers in public service, enter certain professions, or start businesses, hindering their economic prospects and inhibiting their ability to achieve financial stability and upward mobility.

Limited access to affordable higher education also undermines the principle of meritocracy by creating barriers to academic achievement and success based on financial resources rather than merit or ability. Students from affluent backgrounds may have greater access to educational opportunities, including test preparation courses, extracurricular activities, and academic support services, giving them a competitive advantage in college admissions and scholarship competitions. This perpetuates socioeconomic disparities and limits opportunities for individuals from disadvantaged backgrounds to pursue higher education and achieve their full potential.

Addressing limited access to affordable higher education requires comprehensive reforms to make college accessible and affordable for all students. This includes increasing investment in public higher education institutions, expanding need-based financial aid programs, and reducing the reliance on student loans to finance college expenses. Additionally, policymakers can explore innovative solutions such as tuition-free community college programs, income-based repayment plans for student loans, and initiatives to lower the cost of textbooks and course materials.

Promoting access to affordable higher education is essential for expanding opportunities for individual students, strengthening the economy, and fostering social mobility and economic prosperity.

By investing in higher education and removing financial barriers to college attendance, policymakers can help ensure that all individuals have the opportunity to pursue their academic aspirations and achieve their full potential, regardless of their socioeconomic background.

Lack Of Paid Family Leave

The lack of paid family leave in the United States is a significant issue that leaves many workers without essential support during critical life events such as childbirth, adoption, or caring for sick family members. Unlike many other developed nations, the U.S. does not guarantee paid leave for these circumstances, which can have profound implications for individuals and families.

One of the most significant consequences of the absence of paid family leave policies is the perpetuation of gender inequalities in the workforce. Women are disproportionately affected by the lack of paid leave, as they often bear the primary responsibility for caregiving and may face economic pressure to return to work soon after giving birth or adopting a child. This can contribute to gender wage gaps, career interruptions, and limited opportunities for advancement for women in the workforce.

The lack of paid family leave also exacerbates economic insecurity for individuals and families. Without paid leave benefits, workers may be forced to take unpaid time off or exhaust their savings to care for themselves or their loved ones during times of need. This can lead to financial strain, debt, and instability, particularly for low-income workers who may be least able to afford unpaid leave.

Furthermore, the absence of paid family leave policies creates challenges in balancing work and caregiving responsibilities, leading to stress and burnout for workers juggling their professional and personal lives. Without adequate support for caregiving, individuals may face difficult choices between meeting their work obligations and attending to the needs of their families, which can have negative consequences for both their well-being and productivity.

Paid family leave has been shown to have numerous benefits, including improved maternal and child health outcomes, increased workforce participation among women, and greater employee satisfaction and loyalty. By guaranteeing paid leave for workers, policymakers can help address gender inequalities, promote economic security, and support the well-being of families and communities.

Several states and municipalities in the U.S. have implemented their own paid family leave programs. However, a comprehensive federal policy is needed to ensure all workers can access this essential benefit. By enacting paid family leave legislation at the national level, the U.S. can join other developed nations in recognizing the importance of supporting workers during life events and promoting greater equality and prosperity.

Rural Healthcare Access

Rural healthcare access in the United States presents a complex challenge characterized by shortages of healthcare providers, limited availability of medical facilities, and significant travel distances to access care. These disparities in healthcare access contribute to poorer health outcomes and exacerbate health inequities between rural and urban populations.

One of the primary issues affecting rural healthcare access is the shortage of healthcare providers, including physicians, nurses, and specialists. Many rural areas struggle to attract and retain healthcare professionals due to lower salaries, limited career advancement opportunities, and geographic isolation. As a result, residents of rural communities may face difficulties in accessing timely and comprehensive medical care, leading to delayed diagnoses, untreated conditions, and preventable health complications.

The limited availability of medical facilities further compounds the challenges of rural healthcare access. Many rural areas lack hospitals, clinics, and other healthcare facilities, forcing residents to travel long distances for specialized care or emergency services. This can be particularly burdensome for individuals with chronic conditions or mobility limitations, who may face significant barriers to accessing the care they need.

In addition to physical barriers, rural communities often experience socioeconomic challenges that impact healthcare access. Higher rates of poverty, unemployment, and lack of health insurance coverage can limit individuals' ability to afford medical care and preventive services, further exacerbating disparities in health outcomes. Limited access to transportation and internet connectivity may also hinder residents' ability to schedule appointments, access telemedicine services, or obtain health information online.

Addressing rural healthcare access requires a multifaceted approach addressing supply-side and demand-side factors. Strategies to attract and retain healthcare providers in rural areas may include offering loan repayment programs, providing incentives for practicing in underserved communities, and expanding telemedicine and telehealth services to bridge geographic distances. Investing in infrastructure improvements, such as building new medical facilities and expanding transportation networks, can also help improve access to care for rural residents.

Furthermore, addressing socioeconomic determinants of health, such as poverty, education, and housing, is essential for reducing health inequities in rural communities. This may involve expanding access to health insurance coverage, increasing funding for community health centers and safety net programs, and implementing policies to address social and economic disparities.

By addressing the unique challenges of rural healthcare access, policymakers can help ensure that all Americans have equitable access to high-quality medical care, regardless of where they live. This improves rural residents' health outcomes and strengthens communities' overall health and well-being nationwide.

Digital Divide

The digital divide represents a significant disparity in access to and utilization of technology, particularly high-speed internet, across various demographic groups and geographic regions in the United States. This discrepancy in access to digital resources has far-reaching implications, impacting educational opportunities, economic development, and social inclusion for millions of Americans, especially those living in rural and underserved communities.

One of the primary consequences of the digital divide is its impact on educational opportunities. In an increasingly digital world, access to the internet and digital resources is essential for students to participate in online learning, access educational materials, and engage in distance education programs. However, many students, particularly those in rural areas or from low-income households, lack reliable internet connectivity at home, making it challenging to complete assignments, participate in virtual classrooms, or access online educational resources. This hinders their academic progress and exacerbates educational inequalities between students with and without access to digital technology.

Moreover, the digital divide has economic implications, particularly for individuals and communities lacking high-speed internet access. In today's digital economy, accessing online job opportunities, conducting business transactions, and engaging in e-commerce are essential for economic participation and advancement. However, without reliable internet connectivity, individuals in rural and underserved areas may face barriers to accessing employment opportunities, starting businesses, or participating in the digital marketplace. This perpetuates economic disparities and limits economic development in these communities.

Additionally, the digital divide can exacerbate social exclusion and marginalization for individuals who lack access to digital technology. In an increasingly interconnected world, access to the internet and digital communication tools is essential for staying connected with friends and family, accessing social services, and participating in civic life. However, individuals without reliable internet connectivity may face barriers to accessing essential services, participating in virtual social networks, or engaging in online activism and advocacy. This can further isolate and disenfranchise already marginalized communities, exacerbating social inequalities and hindering community development.

Addressing the digital divide requires concerted efforts from policymakers, community leaders, and technology providers to expand access to high-speed internet and digital resources for all Americans. This may involve investing in broadband infrastructure in rural and underserved areas, providing subsidies or incentives for low-income households to access affordable internet service, and promoting digital literacy and skills training programs to empower individuals to fully participate in the digital economy.

By bridging the digital divide, we can create a more equitable and inclusive society where all Americans have the opportunity to thrive in the digital age.

Labor Rights And Worker Protections

Labor rights and worker protections are essential to ensuring fair and dignified treatment for workers in the United States. However, many workers face significant challenges related to inadequate wages, unsafe working conditions, and limited access to essential benefits such as healthcare and paid leave. The erosion of labor unions and weakening of worker protections further exacerbate these issues, leaving many workers vulnerable to exploitation and unfair treatment in the workplace.

One of the primary challenges workers face in the United States is inadequate wages. Despite being one of the wealthiest nations globally, many workers struggle to make ends meet on minimum wage or low-paying jobs. Inadequate wages can lead to financial instability, poverty, and difficulty accessing necessities such as housing, healthcare, and education. Additionally, wage theft and unpaid overtime are common issues faced by workers, further contributing to economic insecurity and inequality.

Unsafe working conditions are another significant concern for workers in the United States. Many workers are exposed to hazardous conditions, such as exposure to toxic chemicals, unsafe machinery, and workplace violence. Without adequate workplace safety regulations and enforcement mechanisms, workers are at risk of injury, illness, and even death. Vulnerable populations, such as immigrant workers and workers in industries such as agriculture and construction, are particularly susceptible to unsafe working conditions.

Limited access to benefits such as healthcare and paid leave also poses challenges for workers in the United States. While access to healthcare is considered a fundamental right, many workers lack health insurance coverage or face barriers to accessing affordable care. Additionally, the absence of paid leave policies means that workers may be forced to choose between their health and financial security when faced with illness or caregiving responsibilities.

The erosion of labor unions and weakening worker protections further compound these challenges. Labor unions are crucial in advocating for workers' rights, negotiating fair wages and benefits, and providing collective bargaining power. However, anti-union policies, aggressive union-busting tactics by employers, and the decline of organized labor have weakened the voice and bargaining power of workers, making it more challenging to address workplace injustices and secure better working conditions.

Addressing the challenges workers face in the United States requires a comprehensive approach prioritizing labor rights and worker protections. This may include strengthening labor laws and enforcement mechanisms, promoting unionization and collective bargaining rights, raising the minimum wage to a living wage, and expanding access to essential benefits such as healthcare and paid leave.

By prioritizing workers' well-being and dignity, policymakers can create a more equitable and just society where all workers are treated fairly and afforded the protections they deserve.

Climate Change Impacts

Climate change poses significant challenges for the United States, impacting various societal and environmental aspects. From extreme weather events to rising sea levels and environmental degradation, the effects of climate change are already being felt across the country. Inadequate action to address these challenges exacerbates community vulnerabilities, threatens public health and safety, and undermines efforts to mitigate the impacts of global warming on future generations.

One of the most visible and immediate impacts of climate change is the increase in the frequency and severity of extreme weather events. Hurricanes, wildfires, floods, and heatwaves have become more frequent and intense, causing widespread destruction, loss of life, and displacement of communities. These extreme weather events threaten public safety and have long-term consequences for infrastructure, agriculture, and natural ecosystems.

Rising sea levels are another consequence of climate change that poses significant risks for coastal communities. As temperatures rise, polar ice caps and glaciers melt, contributing to the expansion of ocean waters. This, combined with the thermal expansion of seawater, results in higher sea levels, leading to coastal erosion, flooding, and saltwater intrusion into freshwater sources. Low-lying coastal regions, including major cities like Miami and New Orleans, are particularly vulnerable to the impacts of sea-level rise, risking billions of dollars in property damage and displacement of populations.

Environmental degradation, including loss of biodiversity, deforestation, and degradation of ecosystems, is exacerbated by climate change. Temperature and precipitation patterns disrupt ecosystems, leading to habitat shifts, loss of species, and reduced resilience to environmental stressors. This threatens biodiversity and ecosystem services and undermines the natural resources and livelihoods of communities dependent on healthy ecosystems for food, water, and economic activities.

Inadequate action to address climate change not only exacerbates these impacts but also undermines efforts to mitigate the effects of global warming on future generations. Without significant reductions in greenhouse gas emissions and concerted efforts to transition to a low-carbon economy, the impacts of climate change will continue to escalate, leading to irreversible damage to ecosystems and exacerbating social and economic inequalities.

Addressing the impacts of climate change requires urgent and ambitious action at local, national, and global levels. This includes reducing greenhouse gas emissions, increasing resilience to climate impacts through adaptation measures, investing in clean energy and sustainable infrastructure, and promoting international cooperation to address the root causes of climate change.

By prioritizing climate action and adopting a holistic approach to sustainability, policymakers can mitigate the worst impacts of climate change and build a more resilient and sustainable future for all.

Disparities In Access To Legal Representation

Disparities in access to legal representation are pervasive issues in the United States, creating significant barriers for many individuals, especially those from low-income and marginalized communities, in navigating the legal system. Limited access to legal aid and representation undermines the principle of equal justice under the law. It perpetuates injustices related to housing, employment, immigration, and other legal matters.

One of the primary challenges individuals seeking legal representation face is the high cost of legal services. Legal fees can be prohibitively expensive, making it difficult for low-income individuals to afford quality legal representation. As a result, many individuals are forced to navigate complex legal processes on their own without the guidance and support of a qualified attorney. This can lead to misunderstandings of legal rights, procedural errors, and unequal outcomes in legal proceedings.

Furthermore, the availability of legal aid and pro bono services is limited, particularly in underserved rural areas and urban neighborhoods with high poverty rates. Legal aid organizations and pro bono attorneys often operate with limited resources and capacity, making it challenging to meet the demand for legal assistance from needy individuals. As a result, many individuals cannot access the legal representation they need to address legal issues such as eviction, debt collection, family law matters, and immigration proceedings.

Additionally, systemic barriers such as language, lack of transportation, and limited awareness of legal rights further compound the challenges individuals seeking legal representation face. Immigrant communities, non-English speakers, and individuals with disabilities are particularly vulnerable to these barriers, which can prevent them from effectively accessing legal services and asserting their rights under the law.

The consequences of limited access to legal representation are profound and far-reaching. Without adequate legal representation, individuals may be unfairly disadvantaged in legal proceedings, leading to unjust outcomes and perpetuating cycles of poverty and inequality. Moreover, disparities in access to legal representation can undermine public trust in the justice system and erode confidence in the rule of law.

Addressing disparities in access to legal representation requires a multifaceted approach that involves expanding funding for legal aid organizations, increasing pro bono participation among attorneys, improving outreach and education efforts to raise awareness of legal rights, and implementing policies to reduce systemic barriers to access.

By prioritizing equal access to justice for all individuals, policymakers can help ensure that the legal system upholds fairness, equality, and the rule of law for all members of society.

Childhood Poverty

Childhood poverty remains a pervasive issue in the United States despite its status as one of the wealthiest nations in the world. Millions of children across the country face the harsh realities of poverty, experiencing food insecurity, inadequate housing, and limited access to healthcare, all of which significantly impact their well-being and prospects.

One of the most visible manifestations of childhood poverty is food insecurity. Many children in low-income households lack consistent access to nutritious and sufficient food, leading to hunger and malnutrition. Food insecurity can have long-term consequences for children's physical and cognitive development, affecting their learning, growth, and thriving ability. The stress and uncertainty of not knowing where their next meal will come from can also affect children's mental and emotional well-being.

Inadequate housing is another significant challenge faced by children living in poverty. Many low-income families struggle to afford safe and stable housing, leading to overcrowded living conditions, substandard housing, and homelessness. These housing challenges can have detrimental effects on children's health, education, and overall quality of life, contributing to increased risk of chronic illnesses, exposure to environmental hazards, and disruptions in schooling.

Access to healthcare is another critical issue for children living in poverty. Many low-income families lack health insurance coverage or face barriers to accessing affordable healthcare services, including preventive care, medical treatments, and prescription medications. As a result, children living in poverty are more likely to experience untreated medical conditions, delayed diagnoses, and limited access to essential healthcare resources, placing them at greater risk of poor health outcomes and lifelong health disparities.

The consequences of childhood poverty extend beyond individual children and families to society as a whole. Children who grow up in poverty face more significant challenges in achieving academic success, securing stable employment, and breaking the cycle of poverty in future generations. Moreover, childhood poverty imposes significant economic costs on society, including lost productivity, increased healthcare spending, and higher rates of crime and incarceration.

Addressing childhood poverty requires a comprehensive and coordinated approach that addresses the root causes of poverty and provides targeted interventions to support children and families in need. This may include policies to increase access to affordable housing, expand access to high-quality early childhood education and childcare, strengthen social safety nets, and improve healthcare services for low-income families.

By investing in the well-being and prospects of children living in poverty, policymakers can help ensure that all children have the opportunity to reach their full potential and lead healthy, fulfilling lives.

Economic Mobility

Economic mobility, once considered a cornerstone of the American dream, has faced significant challenges in recent years, with individuals from low-income backgrounds encountering more significant barriers to upward social and economic mobility. Limited access to quality education, affordable housing, and stable employment opportunities perpetuate cycles of poverty and inequality, hindering the ability of individuals to improve their economic circumstances and achieve upward mobility.

One of the primary factors contributing to declining economic mobility is the unequal access to quality education. Children from low-income families often attend under-resourced schools that lack adequate funding, experienced teachers, and essential resources, placing them at a disadvantage compared to their wealthier peers. As a result, these children are less likely to receive a high-quality education that prepares them for success in higher education and the workforce, limiting their opportunities for upward mobility.

Affordable housing is another critical determinant of economic mobility. Many low-income individuals and families struggle to afford safe and stable housing, leading to housing instability, overcrowded living conditions, and homelessness. Without access to affordable housing, individuals may face increased financial stress, limited opportunities for economic advancement, and barriers to accessing essential services and amenities that support upward mobility.

Stable employment opportunities are essential for economic mobility. Yet, many individuals from low-income backgrounds face challenges in securing and maintaining meaningful employment. Structural barriers such as discrimination, lack of access to transportation, and limited availability of jobs in low-income communities contribute to persistent unemployment and underemployment among marginalized populations. Additionally, the rise of contingent work arrangements, such as temporary and gig work, has further exacerbated economic insecurity and hindered many workers' upward mobility.

The decline in economic mobility has far-reaching consequences for individuals, families, and society. Persistent poverty and inequality limit opportunities for social and economic advancement, perpetuating intergenerational cycles of disadvantage and hindering efforts to achieve greater equality of opportunity. Moreover, declining economic mobility undermines the foundational principles of meritocracy and fairness, eroding public trust in the promise of the American dream and the belief that hard work and talent will lead to success.

Addressing the decline in economic mobility requires a multifaceted approach that addresses the root causes of poverty and inequality while expanding opportunities for upward mobility for all individuals. This may include policies to increase access to high-quality education, expand affordable housing options, promote inclusive economic growth, and strengthen social safety nets to support needy individuals and families.

By investing in pathways to economic mobility, policymakers can help ensure that all individuals have the opportunity to achieve their full potential and contribute to a more equitable and prosperous society.

Disparities In Access To Nutrition

Disparities in access to nutrition represent a significant challenge facing many Americans, especially those living in low-income and marginalized communities. Food insecurity and malnutrition are pervasive issues that affect millions of individuals and families across the country, undermining public health and well-being and exacerbating existing health disparities.

Food insecurity, defined as the lack of consistent access to enough food for an active, healthy life, remains a persistent problem in the United States. Many individuals and families struggle to afford an adequate and nutritious diet, particularly those with limited financial resources. This often results in the reliance on cheap, calorie-dense foods that are high in sugar, fat, and processed ingredients but low in essential nutrients. As a consequence, individuals may suffer from malnutrition, which can lead to a range of health problems, including obesity, diabetes, cardiovascular disease, and developmental issues.

Limited access to nutritious food options, often referred to as food deserts or food swamps, is a crucial contributor to disparities in nutrition. Many low-income communities lack supermarkets and grocery stores that offer fresh, healthy foods such as fruits, vegetables, and whole grains. Instead, residents may rely on convenience stores, fast food outlets, and corner markets that predominantly sell processed, high-calorie foods with little nutritional value. This lack of access to healthy food options perpetuates poor dietary habits. It contributes to the prevalence of diet-related diseases and health disparities in these communities.

The consequences of disparities in access to nutrition extend beyond individual health outcomes to broader societal implications. Chronic diseases related to poor nutrition, such as obesity, diabetes, and heart disease, impose significant economic burdens on healthcare systems and diminish productivity and quality of life for affected individuals. Moreover, the prevalence of food insecurity and malnutrition undermines efforts to promote public health and well-being, hindering progress towards achieving equitable access to healthcare and reducing health disparities across populations.

Addressing disparities in access to nutrition requires a comprehensive and multifaceted approach that addresses the root causes of food insecurity and malnutrition while promoting equitable access to healthy food options for all individuals and communities. This may include policies to increase access to affordable, nutritious foods in underserved areas, support local food systems and community gardens, expand nutrition education and food assistance programs, and address underlying socioeconomic factors contributing to food insecurity, such as poverty, unemployment, and housing instability.

By prioritizing nutrition as a public health priority and implementing evidence-based interventions, policymakers can help ensure that all Americans have access to nutritious food to lead healthy, productive lives.

Housing Discrimination

Housing discrimination remains a significant issue in the United States, perpetuating inequalities and contributing to residential segregation, particularly affecting communities of color. Discriminatory practices such as redlining, housing segregation, and unequal access to affordable housing persist, undermining the principles of fair housing and equal opportunity.

One of the most notorious forms of housing discrimination is redlining, a practice that emerged in the early 20th century and involved the systematic denial of mortgage loans and insurance to residents of predominantly Black and minority neighborhoods. Through redlining, lenders and insurers labeled specific neighborhoods as "high-risk" based on their racial composition, effectively denying residents access to homeownership and perpetuating cycles of disinvestment and decline in these communities.

Housing segregation, both de jure and de facto, also continues to shape residential patterns in many cities and metropolitan areas nationwide. Historically, racially restrictive covenants and discriminatory lending practices enforced segregation, confining communities of color to segregated neighborhoods with limited access to resources and opportunities. While legal segregation has been outlawed, de facto segregation persists due to factors such as income inequality, educational disparities, and implicit bias in housing markets.

Limited access to affordable housing exacerbates housing discrimination and segregation, particularly for low-income individuals and families. Affordable housing options are often concentrated in neighborhoods with higher poverty rates and lower-quality amenities, perpetuating cycles of poverty and limiting opportunities for upward mobility. Discriminatory lending practices, such as predatory lending and subprime mortgages, further exacerbate housing inequalities, disproportionately impacting communities of color and contributing to disparities in homeownership rates and wealth accumulation.

Zoning policies and land-use regulations also play a role in perpetuating housing discrimination and segregation. Exclusionary zoning practices, such as minimum lot sizes and prohibitions on multifamily housing, restrict access to affordable housing in affluent neighborhoods and perpetuate spatial inequalities. Additionally, gentrification and displacement further marginalize communities of color, as rising property values and rents push longtime residents out of their neighborhoods and exacerbate housing affordability challenges.

Addressing housing discrimination requires a comprehensive approach that addresses historical legacies and contemporary manifestations of inequality. This may include strengthening fair housing laws and enforcement mechanisms, promoting affordable housing development and inclusionary zoning policies, investing in community-led revitalization efforts, and addressing underlying systemic factors such as income inequality and racial disparities in education and employment.

By dismantling barriers to fair housing and promoting equitable access to housing opportunities, policymakers can help create more inclusive and resilient communities where everyone has the opportunity to thrive.

Student Achievement Gaps

Student achievement gaps refer to the disparities in academic performance and educational outcomes between different groups of students, often defined by factors such as race, ethnicity, socioeconomic status, and language proficiency. Despite efforts to promote educational equity and excellence, achievement gaps persist in the United States education system, reflecting systemic inequities and barriers to opportunity that disproportionately affect marginalized and underserved communities.

One of the primary factors contributing to student achievement gaps is unequal access to resources and opportunities. Schools serving low-income and minority students - often lack adequate funding, qualified teachers, and educational resources compared to their wealthier counterparts. This resource disparity can lead to differences in the quality of instruction, curriculum offerings, and extracurricular opportunities, ultimately impacting students' academic performance and long-term success.

Cultural biases and stereotypes also play a role in perpetuating student achievement gaps. Teachers and administrators may hold implicit biases that affect their expectations and perceptions of students from different racial, ethnic, and socioeconomic backgrounds. These biases can manifest in differential treatment, lower academic expectations, and limited access to advanced coursework and gifted programs for certain groups of students, contributing to disparities in academic achievement and opportunities for advancement.

Moreover, systemic inequities within the education system, such as tracking and sorting practices, school discipline policies, and standardized testing requirements, can exacerbate achievement gaps and perpetuate inequality. For example, tracking systems that segregate students into different academic tracks based on perceived ability or achievement can limit opportunities for advancement and perpetuate disparities in educational outcomes. Similarly, harsh disciplinary practices, such as zero-tolerance policies and suspensions, disproportionately affect students of color and students with disabilities, further widening achievement gaps and contributing to the school-to-prison pipeline.

Addressing student achievement gaps requires a multifaceted approach that addresses the root causes and consequences of inequality within the education system. This may include increasing funding and resources for schools serving marginalized communities, implementing culturally responsive teaching practices, dismantling tracking systems and promoting inclusive classrooms, reforming school discipline policies to prioritize restorative justice and positive behavior supports, and addressing systemic inequities in access to advanced coursework and college readiness programs.

Furthermore, efforts to address achievement gaps must involve collaboration among educators, policymakers, community leaders, and families to ensure that all students have access to high-quality education and the support they need to succeed.

By promoting educational equity and excellence for all students, regardless of their background or circumstances, we can build a more just and equitable society where everyone can reach their full potential.

Access To Clean Water

Access to clean water is a fundamental human right. Yet, many communities across the United States face challenges accessing safe and reliable drinking water. Despite advances in water infrastructure, aging systems, pollution, and environmental degradation pose significant obstacles to ensuring all Americans have access to clean and safe water, particularly in underserved and rural areas.

One of the primary challenges to clean water access is aging infrastructure. Many water systems in the United States are outdated and need repair or replacement. Aging pipes, treatment plants, and distribution systems are prone to leaks, breaks, and contamination, jeopardizing the quality and reliability of drinking water supplies. In some cases, lead pipes and outdated water treatment facilities contribute to elevated lead and other contaminants in drinking water, posing serious health risks, particularly for children and pregnant women.

Pollution and environmental degradation also threaten water quality and safety in many communities. Industrial pollution, agricultural runoff, and urban runoff can introduce harmful chemicals, toxins, and pathogens into water sources, contaminating drinking water supplies and endangering public health. In addition, factors such as fracking, mining, and deforestation can degrade water quality and disrupt local ecosystems, further exacerbating water-related challenges.

Furthermore, disparities in access to clean water disproportionately affect underserved and marginalized communities, including low-income neighborhoods, communities of color, and rural areas. These communities often lack the resources and political power to address water infrastructure challenges and environmental injustices, leaving them vulnerable to water contamination and health risks.

Addressing the issue of access to clean water requires a comprehensive and equitable approach that prioritizes investments in water infrastructure, pollution prevention, and environmental justice. This may include upgrading and modernizing water treatment plants and distribution systems, replacing lead pipes and outdated infrastructure, implementing stricter regulations to protect water quality, and investing in sustainable water management practices.

Additionally, efforts to ensure clean water access must involve community engagement, public education, and advocacy to empower affected communities and promote environmental justice.

By addressing the root causes of water pollution and infrastructure challenges and prioritizing the needs of underserved communities, we can work towards ensuring that all Americans have access to clean and safe drinking water, regardless of their zip code or socioeconomic status.

Criminalization Of Poverty

The criminalization of poverty refers to the phenomenon where individuals who are experiencing poverty or homelessness are disproportionately targeted and penalized by the criminal justice system for offenses related to their socioeconomic status. In the United States, this issue manifests in various ways, including punitive measures such as fines, fees, and incarceration for activities such as loitering, sleeping in public spaces, or panhandling.

One of how poverty is criminalized is through laws and ordinances that target activities associated with homelessness. For example, many cities have implemented laws prohibiting sleeping in public spaces or panhandling, effectively criminalizing homelessness and pushing individuals experiencing homelessness into the criminal justice system. Instead of addressing the root causes of homelessness, such as the lack of affordable housing and supportive services, these punitive measures perpetuate a cycle of poverty and incarceration, further marginalizing already vulnerable populations.

Additionally, fines and fees for minor infractions disproportionately affect low-income individuals and families who may struggle to afford these financial obligations. Failure to pay fines or appear in court can result in additional penalties, including arrest warrants and incarceration, trapping individuals in a cycle of debt and legal entanglement. This practice, known as "debtors' prison," penalizes poverty and undermines principles of fairness and justice within the legal system.

Moreover, the criminalization of poverty exacerbates systemic injustices and perpetuates social inequality. Research has shown that individuals from low-income and marginalized communities are disproportionately represented in the criminal justice system, facing higher rates of arrest, conviction, and incarceration compared to their wealthier counterparts. This disparity reflects broader socioeconomic inequalities and systemic barriers to opportunity that limit disadvantaged populations' life chances and upward mobility.

Addressing the criminalization of poverty requires a multifaceted approach that addresses the root causes of poverty and homelessness while reforming punitive policies and practices within the criminal justice system. This may include investing in affordable housing, mental health, substance abuse treatment, and supportive services for individuals experiencing homelessness, as well as reforming bail and fines policies to ensure that they do not disproportionately impact low-income individuals. Additionally, efforts to promote economic opportunity, reduce income inequality, and dismantle systemic barriers to social mobility are essential for addressing the underlying drivers of poverty and inequality in society.

Disability Discrimination

Disability discrimination persists as a significant societal challenge, wherein individuals with disabilities encounter barriers and prejudices that impede their full participation in various aspects of life. Despite legal protections such as the Americans with Disabilities Act (ADA), people with disabilities continue to face discrimination and systemic barriers that limit their access to employment, education, transportation, and public accommodations.

One of the primary issues faced by individuals with disabilities is the lack of adequate accommodations in various settings. Many workplaces, educational institutions, public spaces, and transportation systems fail to provide necessary accommodations such as wheelchair ramps, accessible restrooms, or assistive technologies, making it difficult for individuals with disabilities to navigate and access these environments. This lack of accessibility not only limits opportunities for participation but also reinforces social exclusion and marginalization.

Furthermore, stigma and negative attitudes towards disability contribute to discrimination and social barriers faced by individuals with disabilities. Stereotypes and misconceptions about disability often lead to prejudicial treatment, exclusion from social activities, and limited opportunities for employment and advancement. These attitudes not only undermine the dignity and rights of individuals with disabilities but also perpetuate systemic inequalities and barriers to inclusion in society.

Additionally, discrimination in employment remains a significant issue for individuals with disabilities. Despite legal protections against discrimination in hiring and employment practices, many individuals with disabilities face challenges in finding and maintaining employment due to employer biases, lack of accommodations, and inaccessible work environments. This leads to higher rates of unemployment, underemployment, and economic insecurity among people with disabilities, further perpetuating cycles of poverty and exclusion.

Addressing disability discrimination requires comprehensive efforts to promote accessibility, inclusion, and equal opportunities for individuals with disabilities. This includes ensuring that public spaces, transportation systems, educational institutions, and workplaces are fully accessible and accommodating to the needs of people with disabilities. Additionally, efforts to challenge stereotypes, promote awareness, and combat stigma are essential for fostering a more inclusive and equitable society.

Moreover, enforcing existing legal protections and expanding support services for individuals with disabilities, such as vocational training, job placement assistance, and healthcare services, are crucial steps toward addressing systemic barriers and promoting the full participation and integration of people with disabilities in all aspects of society. By working to eliminate discrimination and create a more inclusive society, we can ensure that individuals with disabilities have the same rights, opportunities, and quality of life as their non-disabled peers.

Human Rights Violations

Human rights violations in the United States have been a subject of domestic and international scrutiny, raising concerns about the protection of fundamental rights and liberties for all individuals within the country's borders. While the United States has historically positioned itself as a champion of human rights globally, it has faced criticism for its handling of various issues, including civil liberties, immigrant rights, and indigenous rights.

One of the most prominent human rights concerns in the United States is police brutality, particularly against marginalized communities such as Black Americans and other people of color. Incidents of police violence, including the use of excessive force, racial profiling, and unjustified shootings, have sparked nationwide protests and calls for accountability. The disproportionate impact of police brutality on communities of color reflects broader systemic inequalities and racial biases within law enforcement agencies, highlighting the need for reforms to address police misconduct and ensure equal protection under the law for all individuals.

Additionally, the United States has been criticized for its mass incarceration system, which disproportionately affects low-income communities and communities of color. The war on drugs, mandatory minimum sentencing laws, and racial disparities in the criminal justice system have contributed to the overrepresentation of Black and Hispanic individuals in prisons and jails. This mass incarceration not only violates the rights of individuals to fair and equal treatment but also perpetuates cycles of poverty, disenfranchisement, and social exclusion within affected communities.

Furthermore, the detention of asylum seekers and immigrants in overcrowded and inhumane detention facilities has raised concerns about the treatment of vulnerable populations and the protection of immigrant rights. Reports of substandard living conditions, lack of access to healthcare, and family separation policies have drawn condemnation from human rights organizations and advocates, calling attention to the need for humane and compassionate immigration policies that uphold the dignity and rights of all individuals.

Another area of concern is the protection of indigenous rights, including land rights, environmental justice, and cultural preservation. Indigenous communities in the United States face ongoing challenges related to land dispossession, resource extraction, and environmental degradation, which threaten their way of life and cultural heritage. Efforts to protect indigenous rights and sovereignty are essential for addressing historical injustices and ensuring the well-being and self-determination of indigenous peoples.

Addressing human rights violations in the United States requires a comprehensive approach that addresses systemic inequalities, promotes accountability and transparency in law enforcement and criminal justice systems, and upholds the rights and dignity of all individuals, regardless of race, ethnicity, immigration status, or background. By recognizing and addressing human rights concerns within its borders, the United States can work towards creating a more just, equitable, and inclusive society for all its inhabitants.

Lack Of Affordable Childcare.

The lack of affordable childcare in the United States presents a significant challenge for working families, particularly for women who are disproportionately affected due to traditional caregiving roles. The high cost of childcare places a considerable financial burden on parents, often exceeding the cost of rent or mortgage payments in many parts of the country. This financial strain can force families to make difficult choices, such as forgoing employment opportunities or relying on informal and unregulated childcare arrangements, which may not meet quality and safety standards.

Limited access to affordable childcare hinders workforce participation and economic mobility, particularly for low-income families. Many parents, especially single parents, face barriers to entering or remaining in the workforce due to the lack of affordable childcare options. This not only limits their earning potential but also perpetuates cycles of poverty and dependence on public assistance programs.

Moreover, the lack of affordable childcare contributes to gender inequality in the workforce. Women, who often bear the primary responsibility for childcare,

are disproportionately impacted by the high cost of childcare. The inability to afford quality childcare may force women to reduce their work hours, take lower-paying jobs, or leave the workforce altogether, thus hindering their career advancement and economic independence.

The systemic challenges in supporting working families with affordable childcare are multifaceted. Factors such as inadequate public funding for childcare subsidies, limited availability of childcare providers, and disparities in childcare quality and accessibility contribute to the problem. Additionally, the COVID-19 pandemic has further exacerbated existing childcare challenges, with many childcare facilities closing or operating at reduced capacity due to health and safety concerns.

Addressing the lack of affordable childcare requires a comprehensive approach that involves policymakers, employers, and communities. This includes increasing public investment in childcare subsidies and early childhood education programs, implementing policies that support working families, such as paid family leave and flexible work arrangements, and improving the quality and accessibility of childcare services. By prioritizing affordable childcare as a critical economic and social policy component, the United States can better support working families, promote gender equality, and foster economic mobility for all.

Access To Affordable Prescription Drugs

Access to affordable prescription drugs is a pressing issue in the United States, affecting millions of Americans who struggle to afford necessary medications. The high cost of prescription drugs places a significant financial burden on individuals and families, often forcing them to make difficult choices between purchasing essential medications and meeting other basic needs.

One of the primary drivers of high drug prices is the lack of price regulation in the pharmaceutical industry. Pharmaceutical companies have considerable discretion in setting drug prices, leading to exorbitant prices for many medications, including life-saving drugs for chronic conditions such as diabetes, asthma, and heart disease. The complex drug pricing system, which involves multiple intermediaries such as pharmacy benefit managers and insurers, further obscures pricing transparency and contributes to inflated costs.

Furthermore, many Americans face challenges in accessing prescription medications due to inadequate insurance coverage. High deductibles, copayments, and coverage limitations often leave individuals with significant out-of-pocket expenses for prescription drugs, particularly for specialty medications and brand-name drugs that insurance plans may not cover. For those without insurance, the cost of prescription drugs can be prohibitively expensive, leading to medication non-adherence and adverse health outcomes.

Another barrier to affordable prescription drugs is the limited availability of generic alternatives. Generic drugs are typically less expensive than brand-name drugs. Yet, barriers such as patent protections, regulatory hurdles, and market exclusivity agreements often delay the introduction of generic alternatives, allowing brand-name manufacturers to maintain monopolies and keep prices high.

The consequences of limited access to affordable prescription drugs are far-reaching. Many individuals forgo necessary medications or ration their doses to stretch their supply, putting their health at risk and exacerbating their medical conditions. Others may resort to purchasing medications from unregulated sources or traveling abroad to access lower-cost medications, further compromising their safety and well-being.

Addressing the challenges of access to affordable prescription drugs requires a comprehensive approach that involves government intervention, regulatory reform, and collaboration among stakeholders. Policy solutions may include implementing drug price controls, increasing transparency in drug pricing, facilitating the importation of lower-cost medications, and promoting competition in the pharmaceutical market to expand access to generic alternatives. Additionally, expanding insurance coverage and enhancing prescription drug assistance programs can help alleviate financial burdens for individuals with limited means. By addressing the root causes of high drug prices and ensuring equitable access to affordable medications, the United

States can improve health outcomes, reduce healthcare disparities, and enhance the well-being of its citizens.

Maternal Mortality Rates

Maternal mortality rates in the United States are a critical public health issue, reflecting the number of maternal deaths per 100,000 live births. Despite being a developed nation, the U.S. faces alarmingly high maternal mortality rates compared to other industrialized countries, and significant racial and ethnic disparities exacerbate this disparity.

Black women in the United States are disproportionately affected by maternal mortality, experiencing pregnancy-related complications and death at significantly higher rates than white women. According to statistics, Black women are three to four times more likely to die from pregnancy-related causes than white women. This stark disparity underscores the systemic inequalities and barriers to quality maternal healthcare that persist in the United States.

Several factors contribute to the high maternal mortality rates among Black women, including structural racism, socioeconomic disparities, and inadequate access to healthcare services. Structural racism permeates the healthcare system, leading to biases in medical treatment, differential access to care, and poorer health outcomes for Black women. Socioeconomic factors such as poverty, lack of health insurance, and limited access to prenatal care also play a significant role in increasing the risk of maternal mortality among Black women.

Additionally, Black women often face unique challenges and stressors during pregnancy and childbirth, including discrimination, stress, and trauma, which can contribute to adverse maternal health outcomes. These factors intersect and compound to create a complex web of systemic barriers that undermine the health and well-being of Black mothers.

Addressing the disparities in maternal mortality rates requires a multifaceted approach that addresses the root causes of health inequities and promotes access to quality maternal healthcare for all women. This includes implementing policies to combat systemic racism in healthcare, expanding access to prenatal care and maternal health services, improving cultural competency among healthcare providers, and investing in community-based interventions to support maternal health.

Additionally, efforts to address social determinants of health, such as poverty, housing insecurity, and education, are essential for reducing disparities in maternal mortality rates. By prioritizing maternal health equity and implementing evidence-based interventions, the United States can work towards ensuring that all women have access to safe and equitable maternal healthcare, regardless of race or ethnicity.

Veterans' Mental Health Crisis

The mental health crisis among veterans in the United States is a pressing issue that stems from the unique challenges and experiences they face during and after their military service. Many veterans encounter mental health issues such as post-traumatic stress disorder (PTSD), depression, anxiety, and substance abuse, which can significantly impact their well-being and quality of life.

One of the primary contributing factors to the mental health crisis among veterans is the exposure to traumatic events and experiences during their military service. Combat situations, deployment-related stress, and exposure to violence can lead to the development of PTSD and other mental health conditions. Additionally, veterans may face challenges related to transitioning back to civilian life, including difficulties finding employment, reintegration into their communities, and reconnecting with family and friends.

Despite the prevalence of mental health issues among veterans, many encounter barriers to accessing mental health services and support. The stigma surrounding mental illness, concerns about confidentiality, and cultural barriers within the military community can prevent veterans from seeking help or disclosing their struggles. Additionally, limited access to mental health providers, long wait times for appointments, and challenges navigating the complex healthcare system further hinder veterans' ability to receive timely and effective care.

Furthermore, some veterans may turn to substance abuse or self-medication as a way to cope with their mental health symptoms, which can exacerbate their underlying issues and lead to additional challenges.

Addressing the mental health crisis among veterans requires a comprehensive and holistic approach that prioritizes access to quality mental health care and support services. This includes increasing awareness and reducing stigma surrounding mental illness within the military community, expanding access to mental health screenings and treatment options, and providing culturally competent care that addresses the unique needs of veterans.

Additionally, efforts to improve coordination and collaboration between the Department of Veterans Affairs (VA), community-based organizations, and other healthcare providers are essential for ensuring veterans receive seamless and integrated care for their mental health needs. By investing in early intervention, prevention, and evidence-based treatments, the United States can work towards reducing the prevalence of mental health issues among veterans and improving their overall well-being and quality of life.

Lack Of Paid Sick Leave

The absence of paid sick leave policies in the United States presents a significant challenge for many workers, particularly those in low-wage and precarious employment situations. Without access to paid sick leave, workers are often forced to make difficult decisions regarding their health and financial stability, leading to negative consequences for both individuals and society.

One of the primary concerns associated with the lack of paid sick leave is the public health risk it poses. When workers cannot take time off when they are ill, they are more likely to go to work while sick, increasing the spread of contagious illnesses in the workplace and the community. This can lead to outbreaks of infectious diseases such as influenza and COVID-19, posing risks to public health and placing additional strain on healthcare systems.

Moreover, the absence of paid sick leave policies undermines workplace productivity and efficiency. Sick workers who come to work are often less productive, make more errors, and may take longer to recover from illness, ultimately affecting the overall performance of businesses and organizations. Additionally, when employees come to work sick, presenteeism can lead to further spread of illness among coworkers, creating a cycle of decreased productivity and absenteeism.

Furthermore, the lack of paid sick leave perpetuates economic insecurity for vulnerable workers, particularly those in low-wage jobs or precarious employment situations. For many workers living paycheck to paycheck, taking unpaid time off due to illness can result in financial hardship, including difficulty paying for necessities such as food, housing, and healthcare. This can contribute to a cycle of poverty and economic instability, further exacerbating existing societal inequalities.

Addressing the lack of paid sick leave requires policy interventions at both the federal and state levels. Implementing paid sick leave mandates ensures that workers can take time off when they are ill without fear of financial repercussions. Additionally, incentives for businesses to offer paid sick leave, such as tax credits or subsidies, can encourage employers to adopt more generous leave policies.

By prioritizing the health and well-being of workers and investing in policies that support paid sick leave, the United States can mitigate public health risks, enhance workplace productivity, and promote economic stability for all workers.

Native American Rights And Sovereignty

The struggle for Native American rights and sovereignty in the United States is deeply rooted in a history of colonization, dispossession, and systemic oppression. Despite efforts to address historical injustices, indigenous communities continue to face significant challenges related to land rights, sovereignty, and cultural preservation.

Historical injustices, including forced removal from ancestral lands, the establishment of reservations, and the imposition of assimilation policies such as boarding schools, have had devastating impacts on Native American communities. These policies were often implemented without the consent or consultation of indigenous peoples, leading to the loss of traditional territories, languages, and cultural practices.

One of the central issues facing Native American communities today is the ongoing struggle for land rights and sovereignty. Many indigenous nations assert their inherent right to self-governance and control over their lands and resources. Yet, federal and state governments often undermine their sovereignty. Disputes over land ownership, resource extraction, and environmental protection continue to be sources of conflict between indigenous communities and government authorities.

Additionally, Native American communities continue to face disparities in access to essential services such as healthcare, education, and economic opportunities. Limited access to quality healthcare facilities and culturally competent care contributes to health disparities and higher rates of chronic diseases among indigenous populations. Similarly, inadequate funding for education and economic development programs perpetuates cycles of poverty and inequality in many Native American communities.

Cultural preservation is also a critical issue for indigenous peoples in the United States. Efforts to preserve and revitalize traditional languages, ceremonies, and cultural practices are essential for maintaining the unique identities and cultural heritage of Native American communities. However, these efforts are often hindered by ongoing challenges such as cultural appropriation, lack of funding for cultural preservation initiatives, and limited access to sacred sites and traditional territories.

Addressing the challenges facing Native American communities requires a commitment to upholding indigenous rights, promoting tribal sovereignty, and fostering meaningful consultation and collaboration with indigenous leaders and communities. This includes honoring treaty rights, respecting sacred sites, and ensuring equitable access to resources and opportunities for indigenous peoples.

By centering indigenous voices and perspectives in policy-making processes, the United States can work towards reconciliation and justice for Native American communities.

Youth Homelessness

Youth homelessness is a distressing and persistent issue across the United States, affecting thousands of young people each year. It stems from a complex interplay of factors, including family instability, poverty, housing insecurity, and a lack of supportive services.

Many young people experiencing homelessness come from backgrounds marked by family conflict, abuse, neglect, or parental substance abuse. These factors can lead to strained relationships with family members, making it difficult for youth to find stable housing and support networks.

Economic challenges also play a significant role in youth homelessness. Many young people face financial instability, lack of access to affordable housing, and limited job opportunities, making it difficult to secure stable housing. Additionally, the high cost of housing in many urban areas further exacerbates the problem, forcing youth to resort to unstable living situations such as couch surfing, staying in overcrowded shelters, or sleeping on the streets.

Moreover, the lack of supportive services tailored to the unique needs of homeless youth compounds the issue. Many homeless youth face barriers to accessing healthcare, education, employment, and mental health services, further perpetuating the cycle of homelessness and hindering their ability to achieve stability and self-sufficiency.

The consequences of youth homelessness are profound and far-reaching. Homeless youth are at increased risk of experiencing physical and sexual violence, substance abuse, mental health disorders, and exploitation. They also face significant barriers to educational attainment, with high rates of school dropout and academic underachievement among homeless youth.

Addressing youth homelessness requires a comprehensive approach that addresses its root causes and provides targeted interventions to support vulnerable young people. This includes increasing access to affordable housing, strengthening support systems for at-risk families, expanding outreach and support services for homeless youth, and investing in programs that address the unique needs of this population, such as drop-in centers, transitional housing programs, and wraparound services that provide holistic support for youth experiencing homelessness.

By prioritizing the well-being and stability of young people, communities can work towards ending the cycle of youth homelessness and ensuring that all young people have the opportunity to thrive.

Political Dysfunction

Political dysfunction in the United States has reached alarming levels, characterized by deep-seated polarization, legislative gridlock, and a growing sense of disillusionment among the public. At the heart of this dysfunction is the inability of elected officials to find common ground and work together to address pressing issues facing the nation.

Fueled by ideological divides and partisan rhetoric, political polarization has created an environment where compromise and collaboration are increasingly rare. Politicians often prioritize partisan interests instead of seeking solutions that benefit the country, leading to legislative stalemates and policy inertia.

Gridlock in Congress has become a defining feature of American politics, with important legislation often stalling or blocked altogether. The hyper-partisan atmosphere makes it difficult for lawmakers to reach a consensus on critical issues such as healthcare, immigration, climate change, and economic reform, leaving critical problems unresolved and exacerbating public frustration.

Furthermore, money's political influence has undermined the democratic process, with wealthy special interests wielding disproportionate power and influence over elected officials. The proliferation of corporate PACs, Super PACs, and dark money groups has led to concerns about corruption and the prioritization of narrow interests over the common good.

Gerrymandering, manipulating electoral district boundaries to favor one political party over another, has also distorted the electoral process and contributed to political polarization. By drawing congressional districts to maximize partisan advantage, politicians can effectively choose their voters, rather than voters choosing their representatives, further entrenching incumbents and stifling competition.

Additionally, voter suppression tactics, such as strict voter ID laws, purges of voter rolls, and restrictions on early voting, disproportionately impact marginalized communities and undermine the integrity of the electoral system. These efforts to restrict access to the ballot box disenfranchise millions of eligible voters and undermine the principle of democracy.

Overall, political dysfunction in the United States poses a significant threat to the health of the democratic system and the government's ability to address the needs of the American people effectively.

Addressing these challenges will require bipartisan cooperation, electoral reform, and a renewed commitment to democratic principles and institutions.

Lack Of Comprehensive Immigration Reform

The lack of comprehensive immigration reform in the United States is a pressing issue that has remained unresolved for many years. The complexity of the immigration system, coupled with political gridlock and ideological divides, has hindered efforts to enact meaningful and lasting reform.

One of the central issues in the immigration debate is the status of undocumented immigrants living in the United States. Millions of individuals reside in the country without legal authorization, contributing to economic and social dynamics. However, how to address their presence remains contentious, with divergent views on pathways to legal status, deportation policies, and border security measures.

Family separations at the border have garnered widespread attention and condemnation, highlighting the human cost of stringent immigration enforcement policies. The practice of separating children from their parents as they seek asylum or cross the border irregularly has been met with outrage from humanitarian organizations, lawmakers, and the public, sparking calls for more humane and compassionate immigration policies.

The Deferred Action for Childhood Arrivals (DACA) program, established in 2012, has provided temporary relief from deportation and work authorization for hundreds of thousands of young immigrants brought to the country as children. However, the program has faced legal challenges and uncertainty, leaving DACA recipients in limbo and underscoring the need for legislative action to provide a permanent solution.

The lack of comprehensive immigration reform not only perpetuates uncertainty and fear among immigrant communities but also hampers economic growth and undermines the country's values of inclusivity and opportunity. Immigrants play a vital role in the U.S. economy, contributing to various sectors such as agriculture, healthcare, technology, and entrepreneurship. By providing a pathway to legal status and citizenship for undocumented immigrants, reforming the immigration system can harness the talents and potential of immigrants while ensuring fairness and justice for all.

Efforts to achieve comprehensive immigration reform have been hampered by political polarization, with partisan disagreements over issues such as border security, enforcement measures, and the scope of legalization programs. However, there is growing recognition among lawmakers and stakeholders of the need to address immigration reform comprehensively, balancing border security with humane treatment and providing a path to legal status for undocumented immigrants who contribute to society.

In conclusion, addressing the lack of comprehensive immigration reform requires bipartisan cooperation, empathy, and a commitment to upholding America's diversity, inclusion, and opportunity values.

By reforming the immigration system, the United States can strengthen its economy, uphold its humanitarian principles, and reaffirm its status as a beacon of hope and opportunity for immigrants worldwide.

Crisis In Affordable Housing

The crisis in affordable housing presents a significant challenge for millions of Americans across the country, particularly in urban areas where housing costs have skyrocketed, and wages have failed to keep pace. The shortage of affordable housing options has far-reaching consequences, exacerbating issues of poverty, homelessness, and inequality.

One of the primary drivers of the affordable housing crisis is the rapid increase in housing costs, fueled by rising land prices, construction expenses, and market speculation. As a result, rents have soared to unaffordable levels for many low and moderate-income households, forcing them to allocate a disproportionate amount of their income toward housing expenses.

Gentrification, the process of urban revitalization often accompanied by the displacement of long-time residents, further exacerbates the shortage of affordable housing. As wealthier individuals and developers invest in distressed neighborhoods, property values rise, leading to the eviction of low-income tenants and the loss of affordable rental units.

Government support for affordable housing initiatives has been insufficient to address the growing demand for affordable housing. Federal funding for affordable housing programs has stagnated or declined in recent years, limiting the construction of new affordable units and the preservation of existing ones. Additionally, regulatory barriers and NIMBY (Not In My Backyard) opposition often impede efforts to develop affordable housing projects, further exacerbating the shortage.

The lack of affordable housing has profound consequences for individuals and families struggling to make ends meet. Many are forced to live in overcrowded or substandard housing conditions, compromising their health and well-being. Others face the risk of homelessness, as they are unable to afford rising rents or secure stable housing arrangements.

The affordable housing crisis disproportionately affects marginalized communities, including people of color, immigrants, and individuals with disabilities, who often face additional barriers to accessing safe and affordable housing. Discriminatory practices in the housing market, such as redlining and racial steering, perpetuate inequalities and exacerbate disparities in housing opportunities.

Addressing the affordable housing crisis requires a multi-faceted approach that includes both short-term interventions and long-term systemic reforms. This may involve increasing public investment in affordable housing programs, implementing policies to protect tenants from eviction and displacement, and promoting inclusive zoning practices that encourage affordable housing development in all neighborhoods.

Furthermore, efforts to address the underlying causes of the affordable housing crisis, such as income inequality, stagnant wages, and systemic racism, are essential for achieving lasting solutions. By prioritizing affordable housing as a fundamental human right and investing in policies that ensure access to safe and stable housing for all, society can work towards building more equitable and inclusive communities.

Lack Of Accessible Transportation

The lack of accessible transportation in many communities across the United States poses significant challenges for various segments of the population, including individuals with disabilities, seniors, and low-income residents. Access to reliable and affordable transportation is essential for individuals to access essential services, employment opportunities, education, healthcare, and social activities. However, barriers to transportation access contribute to mobility limitations and restrict opportunities for social and economic participation.

One of the primary challenges is the limited availability and accessibility of public transit systems in many communities. Public transportation options may be scarce or non-existent in rural and underserved urban neighborhoods, leaving residents reliant on personal vehicles or costly alternative transportation methods. Even in areas with public transit, inadequate infrastructure, such as inaccessible bus stops, lack of ramps or elevators in subway stations, and poorly maintained sidewalks, can pose significant barriers for individuals with mobility impairments.

Furthermore, disparities in transportation services exacerbate inequities in access to essential resources and opportunities. Low-income neighborhoods and communities of color are disproportionately underserved by public transit systems, leading to longer commute times, higher transportation costs, and limited access to jobs, education, and healthcare facilities. This lack of access perpetuates cycles of poverty and exacerbates social and economic disparities within communities.

The lack of accessible transportation options further restricts the mobility and independence of individuals with disabilities. Many public transit systems lack features such as wheelchair ramps, audible announcements, and priority seating, making it difficult for individuals with mobility impairments or visual or hearing impairments to use public transportation safely and effectively. As a result, individuals with disabilities may face significant challenges in accessing essential services and participating fully in community life.

Addressing the lack of accessible transportation requires a comprehensive approach that considers the diverse needs of all community members. This may involve investing in public transit infrastructure improvements, expanding transit services to underserved areas, and implementing policies to ensure accessibility and inclusivity for individuals with disabilities. Additionally, initiatives such as paratransit services, rideshare programs, and subsidies for low-income individuals can help bridge transportation gaps and improve mobility for vulnerable populations.

Community engagement and collaboration are essential for identifying transportation needs, prioritizing investments, and implementing solutions that enhance accessibility and equity. By working together to remove barriers to transportation access, communities can create more inclusive and connected environments where all residents can thrive and participate fully in society.

Exploitation Of Immigrant Labor

The exploitation of immigrant labor is a concerning issue that persists in the United States, with immigrant workers frequently facing various forms of abuse and mistreatment in the workplace. This exploitation takes many forms, including wage theft, unsafe working conditions, and retaliation for organizing or asserting their rights.

One of the primary factors contributing to the vulnerability of immigrant workers is their legal status. Undocumented immigrants, in particular, often live and work in the shadows due to their unauthorized status, which leaves them afraid to report abuses or seek recourse for violations of their rights. Employers may exploit this fear of deportation to subject immigrant workers to substandard wages, long hours, and hazardous working conditions without fear of repercussions.

Even immigrant workers with legal status, such as those holding temporary visas or work permits, may face exploitation and abuse in the workplace. Employers may rely on sponsorship or visa sponsorship to threaten deportation or revoke their legal status if they speak out against labor violations or attempt to organize for better working conditions.

Wage theft is a common form of exploitation experienced by immigrant workers, wherein employers withhold or underpay wages for work performed. This can take various forms, including failure to pay minimum wage, unpaid overtime, illegal deductions from paychecks, and nonpayment of wages altogether. Immigrant workers, especially those with limited English proficiency or unfamiliarity with labor laws, may be particularly susceptible to wage theft and may not know how to assert their rights or seek legal redress.

Unsafe working conditions are another significant concern for immigrant workers, who may be employed in industries such as construction, agriculture, or manufacturing, where workplace hazards are prevalent. Employers may cut corners on safety measures or fail to provide adequate training and protective equipment, putting immigrant workers at risk of injury, illness, or even death on the job.

Retaliation against immigrant workers who speak out against labor abuses or attempt to organize for better working conditions is also common. Employers may threaten to report undocumented workers to immigration authorities, fire workers who raise concerns about safety or pay, or engage in other forms of retaliation to silence dissent and maintain control over the workforce.

Addressing the exploitation of immigrant labor requires a multi-faceted approach that involves strengthening labor protections, enhancing enforcement of existing laws, and providing pathways to legal status for undocumented immigrants. It also requires fostering a workplace rights awareness and empowerment culture among immigrant workers, ensuring they know their rights and have the resources and support they need to assert them without fear of reprisal. Additionally, efforts to combat discrimination and xenophobia in society at large are essential for creating a more inclusive and equitable environment where all workers are treated with dignity and respect, regardless of their immigration status.

Erosion Of Public Trust In Government

The erosion of public trust in government institutions is a complex and multifaceted issue that has become increasingly prevalent in the United States. Various factors contribute to this decline in trust, including scandals, corruption, and perceived inefficiencies in government operations, all of which foster feelings of skepticism and disillusionment among citizens.

Scandals involving elected officials or government agencies can significantly undermine public trust in government. Instances of unethical behavior, misuse of taxpayer funds, or abuse of power by politicians or government officials can erode confidence in the integrity and accountability of the government. High-profile scandals often receive extensive media coverage, further amplifying public perception of government incompetence or corruption.

Corruption within government institutions is another significant driver of public distrust. When citizens perceive that elected officials or government employees are acting in their self-interest rather than serving the public good, it can lead to feelings of betrayal and cynicism. Corruption may manifest in various forms, including bribery, kickbacks, nepotism, and cronyism, undermining the fairness and legitimacy of government decision-making processes.

Perceived inefficiencies in government operations can also contribute to the erosion of public trust. When citizens feel that government agencies are bureaucratic, unresponsive, or ineffective in addressing pressing issues, they may lose faith in the government's ability to fulfill its responsibilities and meet the needs of the people. Lengthy delays in delivering services, bureaucratic red tape, and instances of government incompetence can all fuel perceptions of government incompetence and contribute to frustration and disillusionment.

The erosion of public trust in government has significant implications for democratic governance and civic engagement. When citizens lose confidence in their government, they may become disengaged from the political process, leading to decreased voter turnout, reduced participation in civic activities, and weakening democratic institutions. Additionally, low levels of trust in government can hinder the government's ability to effectively address societal challenges and implement meaningful policy reforms, as citizens may be less willing to support or cooperate with government initiatives.

Addressing the erosion of public trust in government requires concerted efforts to promote transparency, accountability, and integrity in government institutions. This includes implementing measures to prevent corruption, strengthen ethics regulations, and improve the responsiveness and efficiency of government services. Building trust also requires open and honest communication between government officials and the public and meaningful opportunities for citizen participation in decision-making processes. Ultimately, rebuilding public trust in government is essential for maintaining a healthy and vibrant democracy where citizens have confidence in their elected leaders and government institutions.

Childhood Obesity And Nutrition

Childhood obesity and nutrition represent a critical public health issue in the United States, posing significant challenges to the well-being of children and adolescents. The prevalence of childhood obesity has reached alarming levels, with adverse consequences for physical health, mental well-being, and long-term quality of life.

One of the primary factors contributing to childhood obesity is the consumption of unhealthy diets high in processed foods, sugar, and unhealthy fats. These dietary patterns, often lacking fruits, vegetables, and whole grains, contribute to excessive calorie intake and weight gain. Additionally, the widespread availability of fast food, sugary beverages, and snacks high in calories and low in nutritional value further exacerbates the problem.

Inadequate physical activity levels also play a significant role in the obesity epidemic among children and adolescents. Factors such as increased screen time, sedentary behaviors, and limited access to safe outdoor spaces for play contribute to decreased physical activity levels. The decline in physical education programs in schools and reduced opportunities for recreational activities further compound the issue.

Furthermore, socioeconomic factors, including limited access to affordable, nutritious foods and disparities in healthcare access, contribute to the disparities in childhood obesity rates observed among different demographic groups. Children from low-income families and marginalized communities are disproportionately affected by obesity due to these systemic inequalities.

Childhood obesity not only increases the risk of immediate health problems such as type 2 diabetes, cardiovascular disease, and hypertension but also has long-term implications for overall health and well-being. Obese children are more likely to experience bullying, low self-esteem, and mental health issues, further highlighting the multifaceted nature of the obesity epidemic.

Addressing childhood obesity and promoting nutrition education and healthy lifestyles are essential for public health initiatives to combat this epidemic. Strategies to prevent and reduce childhood obesity include promoting healthy eating habits, increasing access to nutritious foods, implementing comprehensive physical education programs in schools, and creating supportive environments that encourage physical activity.

Furthermore, fostering collaboration among policymakers, healthcare providers, educators, parents, and community stakeholders is crucial for implementing effective interventions and policies to address the root causes of childhood obesity. By prioritizing the health and well-being of children and investing in preventive measures, we can ensure a healthier future for generations to come.

Crisis In Affordable Childcare

The crisis in affordable childcare presents a significant challenge for families across the United States. It impacts parents' ability to balance work and family responsibilities while ensuring the well-being and development of their children. Several factors contribute to this crisis, including high childcare costs, limited availability of affordable options, and disparities in childcare quality.

One of the primary issues facing parents is the high cost of childcare. In many parts of the country, childcare expenses consume a significant portion of families' budgets, rivaling housing and healthcare costs. The childcare expense can be particularly burdensome for low-income families, who may struggle to afford quality care while meeting other basic needs.

The limited availability of affordable childcare options further compounds the problem. In some areas, a shortage of licensed childcare providers leads to long waitlists and limited access to care for needy families. Rural communities, in particular, may face challenges in accessing quality childcare due to geographic isolation and fewer available providers.

Disparities in childcare quality also contribute to the crisis. While some families may have access to high-quality early childhood education programs that promote children's development and school readiness, others may be limited to informal or unregulated care arrangements that lack educational enrichment and safety standards.

The affordability and availability of childcare services directly impact parents' workforce participation and economic stability. Many parents, especially mothers, must choose between staying in the workforce and caring for their children. For some families, the cost of childcare may exceed the parent's income, making it financially untenable to continue working.

The lack of affordable childcare options disproportionately affects women, who often bear the primary responsibility for caregiving. The childcare crisis contributes to gender inequalities in the workforce, hindering women's career advancement and economic independence. Additionally, it perpetuates systemic barriers to gender equality by reinforcing traditional gender roles and expectations.

Addressing the crisis in affordable childcare requires a multifaceted approach that involves policymakers, employers, childcare providers, and community stakeholders. Solutions may include increasing public investment in childcare subsidies and assistance programs, expanding access to high-quality early childhood education, and implementing policies that support work-life balance for parents, such as paid family leave and flexible work arrangements.

Furthermore, efforts to professionalize the childcare workforce, improve wages and benefits for childcare providers, and increase regulatory oversight can help ensure that all children have access to safe, nurturing, and developmentally appropriate care. By prioritizing investments in early childhood education and care, society can support the well-being of children and families while promoting economic opportunity and social equity.

Animal Welfare Concerns

Factory farming, also known as industrial agriculture, is a system of intensive animal agriculture that raises significant concerns about animal welfare in the United States. In these large-scale operations, animals are often confined in crowded and unnatural conditions, deviating from their natural behaviors and environments. This confinement can lead to a host of issues that compromise the well-being of the animals.

One of the primary concerns with factory farming is the overcrowding of animals in small spaces. This crowding limits their movement and creates a stressful and uncomfortable environment. Pigs, chickens, and cows are often kept in confined spaces where they cannot engage in natural behaviors such as foraging, grazing, or socializing. For example, in the poultry industry, chickens are commonly housed in battery cages that are so small they can barely move, let alone spread their wings. This lack of space and freedom of movement can lead to muscle and bone issues and psychological stress.

Another common practice in factory farming is the routine use of antibiotics and growth hormones. These substances are often administered to promote rapid growth and prevent the spread of diseases in crowded conditions. However, the overuse of antibiotics can lead to the development of antibiotic-resistant bacteria, posing risks to both animal and human health.

In addition to overcrowding and the use of antibiotics, factory farming also involves various practices that are considered detrimental to animal welfare. For example, beak trimming (debeaking) in the poultry industry is a common practice to prevent birds from injuring each other due to stress-induced pecking. This procedure involves cutting or burning off a portion of the bird's beak, which can cause pain and long-term health issues.

Similarly, tail docking is often performed on pigs in factory farms to prevent tail biting. This behavior can arise from stress and overcrowding. Tail docking involves cutting off a portion of the pig's tail without anesthesia, leading to pain and potential complications.

The conditions in factory farms can also contribute to the spread of diseases among animals. The proximity of animals in these operations provides ideal conditions for the rapid transmission of diseases, which can devastate animal populations.

Critics of factory farming argue that these practices prioritize efficiency and profit over the well-being of the animals. They argue for more humane and sustainable farming practices, prioritizing the Five Freedoms - freedom from hunger and thirst, discomfort, pain, injury, or disease, freedom to express normal behavior, and freedom from fear and distress.

Improving animal welfare in factory farming includes advocating for better living conditions, reducing antibiotic use, and promoting alternative farming methods such as pasture-based systems. Some consumers also support farms that adhere to higher animal welfare standards, such as those certified by organizations like Certified Humane or Animal Welfare Approved.

In conclusion, factory farming raises significant concerns about animal welfare in the United States. The practices of overcrowding, routine antibiotic use, and procedures such as beak trimming and tail docking are all issues that compromise the well-being of animals. Efforts to address these concerns focus on promoting more humane and sustainable farming practices that prioritize the health and welfare of the animals.

Lack Of Universal Healthcare

The lack of universal healthcare in the United States is a longstanding issue that has profound implications for individuals and families. Unlike many other developed nations, the U.S. does not have a universal healthcare system, meaning that access to healthcare services is often tied to employment or private insurance. This system leaves millions of Americans without adequate or affordable healthcare coverage, leading to various challenges and disparities.

One of the primary consequences of the lack of universal healthcare is the presence of significant health disparities. Without access to regular and preventive care, individuals are more likely to develop chronic conditions that go untreated, leading to poorer health outcomes. Those uninsured or underinsured may delay seeking medical attention due to financial concerns, resulting in more advanced and costly treatments when conditions become severe.

Financial burdens related to healthcare costs are a significant concern for many Americans. High deductibles, copayments, and out-of-pocket expenses can create substantial financial strain, even for those with insurance. Medical bills are a leading cause of bankruptcy in the U.S., highlighting the financial vulnerability faced by individuals and families when confronted with severe illness or injury.

The lack of universal healthcare also affects access to essential medical services. In rural areas and underserved communities, healthcare facilities may be scarce or inaccessible, exacerbating disparities in healthcare access. Additionally, specific populations, such as undocumented immigrants, may face significant barriers to accessing care due to legal status or lack of insurance coverage.

For many Americans, healthcare coverage is tied to employment, creating challenges during job loss or transition. Losing a job - often means losing health insurance coverage, leaving individuals and families without a safety net during times of need. This link between employment and healthcare also limits job mobility and entrepreneurship, as individuals may hesitate to leave a job with healthcare benefits.

The COVID-19 pandemic further underscored the shortcomings of the U.S. healthcare system. The pandemic highlighted the vulnerabilities of those without health insurance and the strain on hospitals and healthcare providers. Many uninsured individuals faced barriers to testing, treatment, and vaccination, leading to unequal outcomes in the face of a public health crisis.

Efforts to address the lack of universal healthcare in the U.S. have been ongoing for years. Proposals for universal healthcare, such as a single-payer system or a public option, aim to provide comprehensive coverage to all Americans regardless of employment status or income. These proposals often emphasize the potential cost savings, improved health outcomes, and equitable access to care that could result from a universal healthcare system.

In conclusion, the lack of universal healthcare in the United States has far-reaching consequences. It perpetuates health disparities, creates financial burdens for individuals and families, limits access to essential services, and hampers economic mobility. Addressing this issue requires thoughtful policy solutions prioritizing equitable access to healthcare as a fundamental right for all Americans.

Urban Sprawl And Environmental Degradation

Urban sprawl, characterized by cities' expansion into suburban and rural areas, has been a persistent challenge in many American cities. It leads to environmental degradation and a host of related issues. Unchecked development and unplanned growth patterns contribute to various environmental problems, from the loss of green spaces and wildlife habitats to increased pollution and strain on natural resources.

One of the primary consequences of urban sprawl is the loss of valuable green spaces. As cities expand outward, they often encroach upon undeveloped land, forests, wetlands, and farmland. These green spaces play crucial roles in maintaining biodiversity, providing wildlife habitats, and offering residents recreational opportunities. However, when these areas are converted into urban developments, ecosystems are fragmented, and biodiversity is lost.

Additionally, urban sprawl contributes to increased pollution and environmental degradation. The reliance on automobiles as the primary mode of transportation in sprawling cities leads to more significant vehicle emissions, air pollution, and traffic congestion. The need for longer commutes from suburban areas to urban centers also results in higher fuel consumption and carbon emissions. This not only contributes to local air quality issues but also contributes to climate change on a broader scale.

Furthermore, expanding impervious surfaces such as roads, parking lots, and buildings in sprawling cities exacerbates stormwater runoff and water pollution issues. Rainwater cannot infiltrate the ground naturally, leading to increased flooding, erosion, and contamination of water bodies with pollutants like oil, chemicals, and sediment.

Inadequate urban planning strategies and zoning regulations often fail to address these environmental concerns effectively. The lack of mixed land use, walkable neighborhoods, and public transportation options in sprawling cities further perpetuates automobile dependence. It contributes to urban areas' environmental footprint.

Efforts to promote sustainability and protect natural resources in the face of urban sprawl require comprehensive urban planning and innovative growth strategies. This includes prioritizing infill development and revitalizing existing urban areas, promoting mixed-use developments that combine residential, commercial, and recreational spaces, and investing in public transportation and active transportation infrastructure such as bike lanes and sidewalks.

Green infrastructure, such as green roofs, rain gardens, and permeable pavements, can help manage stormwater and reduce the impact of impervious surfaces. Conservation easements and land-use policies can protect critical green spaces and wildlife habitats from development.

In conclusion, urban sprawl poses significant challenges to environmental sustainability in American cities. Addressing these challenges requires a holistic approach that balances growth with environmental conservation, promotes efficient land use, reduces automobile dependence, and prioritizes the preservation of green spaces and natural resources. By implementing innovative growth strategies and investing in sustainable urban planning, cities can mitigate the negative impacts of urban sprawl and create healthier, more livable communities for current and future generations.

Fossil Fuel Dependency

In the energy production and environmental stewardship puzzle, the United States' continued reliance on fossil fuels represents a stubbornly entrenched piece with far-reaching implications for the environment and future generations. Despite growing awareness of the adverse effects of fossil fuel dependency, the nation's slow transition to cleaner energy sources remains a critical challenge.

Fossil fuels, including coal, oil, and natural gas, have long been the backbone of America's energy infrastructure, powering industries, transportation, and households. However, this reliance comes at a significant cost. Burning fossil fuels releases greenhouse gases such as carbon dioxide into the atmosphere, contributing to climate change and global warming. The extraction and processing of these fuels also lead to environmental pollution, air and water contamination, and ecological degradation.

Despite these well-documented consequences, limited investment in renewable energy alternatives has impeded progress toward a sustainable future. The United States has vast renewable energy potential, from solar and wind to geothermal and hydroelectric power. Yet, transitioning to these cleaner sources has been slow compared to other developed nations.

Resistance to change, often fueled by economic interests and political considerations, further complicates efforts to wean the nation off fossil fuels. Industries tied to the extraction and production of fossil fuels wield considerable influence, advocating for policies that maintain the status quo. Additionally, concerns about job loss in traditional fossil fuel sectors and the perceived economic risks of transitioning to renewables have slowed the momentum for change.

The challenge lies in balancing economic interests with environmental imperatives in the energy policy puzzle. While the impacts of fossil fuel dependency are clear, the path to a sustainable future is fraught with complexities. Efforts to mitigate climate change and promote sustainability require a holistic approach, including robust investments in renewable energy infrastructure, incentives for clean energy adoption, and policies that facilitate a just transition for workers and communities dependent on fossil fuel industries.

As the world grapples with the urgent need to reduce carbon emissions and mitigate the effects of climate change, the United States stands at a pivotal juncture. Today's energy policy decisions will shape the nation's environmental legacy, economic competitiveness, and resilience in a rapidly evolving global landscape. In this energy transition puzzle, the imperative is to move decisively towards a future powered by clean, renewable energy sources, fostering a sustainable and thriving planet for generations to come.

Cybersecurity Threats

Cybersecurity threats have become a pressing concern for the United States, with various malicious actors posing risks to critical infrastructure, government agencies, businesses, and individuals. These threats come from various sources, including foreign governments, criminal organizations, hacktivists, and individual hackers, and they target a wide range of sectors, from finance and healthcare to energy and transportation.

One of the most significant cybersecurity threats is the potential for cyber attacks on critical infrastructure. Vital systems such as power grids, water supplies, transportation networks, and communication systems are increasingly connected to the internet, making them vulnerable to cyber-attacks. A successful attack on critical infrastructure could have severe consequences, disrupting essential services, causing economic damage, and even posing risks to public safety.

Government agencies at all levels, from federal to local, are also frequent targets of cyber attacks. Hackers may seek access to sensitive information, disrupt operations, or undermine public trust in government institutions. Attacks on government networks can compromise national security, intelligence gathering, and diplomatic efforts.

The private sector is another primary target for cyber attacks, especially industries that handle sensitive information, such as financial institutions, healthcare providers, and technology companies. Cyber attacks on businesses can result in financial losses, data breaches, intellectual property theft, and reputation damage. Small and medium-sized enterprises (SMEs) are particularly vulnerable due to limited resources for cybersecurity measures.

Individuals are not immune to cybersecurity threats either. Personal data breaches, identity theft, phishing scams, ransomware attacks, and other cyber crimes can devastate individuals' finances, privacy, and peace of mind. Cyber attacks on individuals may target personal computers, smartphones, social media accounts, or online banking platforms.

The evolving nature of cybersecurity threats poses challenges for defense and response efforts. Threat actors constantly adapt their tactics, techniques, and procedures (TTPs) to evade detection and exploit vulnerabilities. Advanced persistent threats (APTs) from nation-state actors can be particularly sophisticated and challenging to detect.

To address these cybersecurity challenges, the United States government, private sector, and individuals must adopt a multi-faceted approach:

Enhanced Cybersecurity Measures

Organizations and individuals should implement robust cybersecurity measures like firewalls, antivirus software, encryption, multi-factor authentication, and regular software updates. Security awareness training can help employees recognize and avoid phishing attacks and other social engineering tactics.

Public-Private Collaboration

Collaboration between government agencies and private sector entities is crucial for sharing threat intelligence, best practices, and resources. Public-private partnerships can improve incident response capabilities and strengthen defenses against cyber attacks.

Regulatory Frameworks

Effective cybersecurity regulations and standards can incentivize businesses to invest in cybersecurity measures and ensure critical infrastructure protection. Compliance with regulations such as the Health Insurance Portability and Accountability Act (HIPAA) and the Payment Card Industry Data Security Standard (PCI DSS) can help safeguard sensitive data.

International Cooperation

Borders do not limit cyber threats, so international cooperation is essential for combating cyber attacks. Agreements on cybersecurity norms, information sharing, and mutual assistance can enhance global cybersecurity resilience.

Research and Development

Continued investment in cybersecurity research and development is crucial for staying ahead of emerging threats. Artificial intelligence (AI), machine learning, and behavioral analytics can improve threat detection and response capabilities.

In conclusion, cybersecurity threats pose significant risks to national security, economic stability, and individual privacy in the United States. Addressing these threats requires a comprehensive and collaborative approach involving government, private sector, and individual efforts to enhance cybersecurity measures, share threat intelligence, establish regulatory frameworks, promote international cooperation, and invest in research and development. By working together, stakeholders can better defend against cyber attacks and protect modern society's digital infrastructure.

Lack Of Access To Mental Healthcare

Access to mental healthcare remains a significant challenge for many Americans, with several barriers preventing individuals from receiving the support and treatment they need. These barriers include limited availability of mental health providers, high costs of services, and pervasive stigma surrounding mental illness.

One of the primary challenges is the shortage of mental health professionals, particularly in rural and underserved areas. Many regions nationwide lack adequate psychiatrists, psychologists, counselors, and other mental health providers. This shortage makes it difficult for individuals in these areas to access timely and quality mental healthcare services. Even in urban areas where providers are more plentiful, there can still be long appointment waits, further delaying care.

The cost of mental healthcare services is another significant barrier. Many individuals do not have adequate insurance coverage for mental health treatment, or they may face high out-of-pocket costs even with insurance. This financial burden can deter people from seeking help or continuing with treatment, especially if they need ongoing therapy or medication.

The stigma surrounding mental illness also plays a role in limiting access to care. Despite progress in raising awareness and reducing stigma, many individuals still feel shame or embarrassment about seeking mental health treatment. This stigma can prevent people from discussing their mental health concerns with family, friends, or healthcare providers. Fear of judgment or discrimination may lead individuals to suffer in silence rather than seeking the help they need.

The lack of access to mental health care has significant consequences for individuals and communities. Untreated mental health conditions can have a profound impact on a person's overall well-being, affecting their ability to function in daily life, maintain relationships, and perform at work or school. Without proper treatment, mental health conditions can worsen over time, leading to more severe symptoms and an increased risk of crises such as suicide.

Furthermore, the lack of access to mental healthcare contributes to broader societal issues such as homelessness, substance abuse, and involvement with the criminal justice system. Many individuals with untreated mental illness end up in emergency rooms, jails, or on the streets, where their conditions often go unaddressed or worsen.

Addressing the lack of access to mental healthcare requires a multi-faceted approach:

Increasing Mental Health Providers

Efforts to train and recruit more mental health professionals, especially in underserved areas, are essential. This includes expanding mental health training programs, offering incentives for providers to work in rural and underserved communities, and supporting telehealth services to reach individuals in remote areas.

Improving Insurance Coverage

Policies that improve insurance coverage for mental health services, such as parity laws requiring equal coverage for mental and physical health, can help reduce financial barriers to care. Expanding Medicaid coverage in states that have not done so can also improve access for low-income individuals.

Reducing Stigma

Continued efforts to raise awareness and reduce the stigma surrounding mental illness are crucial. Education campaigns, community events, and media representation that promote understanding and acceptance of mental health conditions can encourage more people to seek help without fear of judgment.

Integrated Care Models

Integrating mental health services into primary care settings can make it easier for individuals to access mental healthcare. This approach allows for earlier detection and treatment of mental health conditions during routine medical visits.

Community-Based Support

Investing in community-based mental health services, such as peer support programs, crisis hotlines, and mental health clinics, can provide crucial resources for individuals who may not have access to traditional mental health providers.

In conclusion, the lack of access to mental healthcare in the United States is a complex issue with far-reaching consequences. Addressing this challenge requires a comprehensive approach that involves increasing the number of mental health providers, improving insurance coverage, reducing stigma, implementing integrated care models, and investing in community-based support services. By addressing these barriers, more individuals can receive the mental healthcare they need to lead healthy and fulfilling lives.

Erosion Of Voting Rights

The erosion of voting rights in the United States has been a persistent issue, marked by various challenges that threaten the fundamental principles of democracy and equal representation. Several factors contribute to this erosion, including voter suppression tactics, gerrymandering, and restrictions on access to polling places.

Voter Suppression Tactics

Voter suppression tactics are deliberate efforts to prevent certain groups of people from exercising their right to vote. These tactics can include strict voter ID laws, purging voter rolls, reducing early voting hours, and closing polling places in minority and low-income neighborhoods. These measures disproportionately affect marginalized communities, making it harder for them to cast their ballots.

Gerrymandering

Gerrymandering is the manipulation of electoral district boundaries to benefit a particular political party or group. Politicians redraw district lines to consolidate their power, often diluting the voting power of minority communities or spreading out opposition voters to minimize their impact. This practice distorts the democratic process by allowing elected officials to choose their voters rather than vice versa.

Restrictions on Access to Polling Places

Access to polling places has become increasingly restricted in many areas, particularly marginalized communities. Polling places may be closed or moved without adequate notice, creating confusion and making it harder for people to vote, especially those without reliable transportation. Long lines at polling places discourage voter turnout, particularly for individuals who cannot afford to take time off work or stand in line for hours.

Disenfranchisement of Minority and Low-Income Voters

These challenges disproportionately affect minority voters, low-income individuals, and communities of color. Historical and systemic barriers, such as voter suppression laws and discriminatory practices, have made it harder for these groups to exercise their right to vote. Additionally, strict voter ID laws and proof of citizenship requirements can present significant hurdles for individuals who may not have access to the necessary documents.

MAKING AMERICA GREAT ALTOGETHER - CALL TO ACTION

The impact of these challenges is significant and far-reaching:

Undermining Democracy

The erosion of voting rights undermines the very foundation of democracy. When certain groups of people are systematically disenfranchised, it distorts the representation of the electorate and skews political outcomes.

Unequal Representation

Gerrymandering distorts electoral districts, resulting in unequal representation. Politicians may cater to the interests of their party's base rather than the broader population, leading to policies that do not reflect the needs or preferences of all constituents.

Reduced Voter Turnout

Voter suppression tactics and barriers to voting can lead to reduced voter turnout, particularly among marginalized communities. When people feel their voices are not heard or their votes do not matter, they are less likely to participate in the electoral process.

Diminished Trust in the Electoral System

When people perceive that the electoral system is rigged or biased against them, they can diminish their trust in the democratic process. This lack of trust can have long-term consequences for civic engagement and participation.

Addressing the erosion of voting rights requires a multifaceted approach:

Voting Rights Legislation

Congress can pass legislation to protect voting rights, such as the Voting Rights Act, which prohibits discriminatory voting practices. Strengthening and enforcing such laws can help prevent voter suppression tactics.

Ending Gerrymandering

States can implement independent redistricting commissions to draw electoral district boundaries reasonably and without political bias. This would help ensure that all voters have equal representation.

Expanding Access to Voting

Early voting, mail-in voting, and online voter registration can make it easier for people to participate in elections. Ensuring an adequate number of polling places and polling hours is also crucial.

Education and Outreach

Public education campaigns can help inform voters about their rights and how to navigate the voting process. Outreach efforts to marginalized communities can ensure they know their voting options and have the necessary resources to participate.

In conclusion, the erosion of voting rights in the United States is a pressing issue that requires attention and action. By addressing voter suppression tactics, ending gerrymandering, expanding access to voting, and promoting education and outreach, we can work towards a more inclusive and representative democracy.

Cultural Divide

The cultural divide in the United States has become more pronounced in recent years, creating perceptions of societal fragmentation and decline. This divide is characterized by polarized debates over identity, values, and the role of government, leading to a sense of disunity and alienation among various segments of the population. Several key issues, including immigration, gun violence, and LGBTQ+ rights, have been particularly contentious and have highlighted deep-seated divisions within American society.

Immigration

Immigration has long been a divisive issue in the United States, with debates centering on issues such as border security, pathways to citizenship, and the treatment of undocumented immigrants. Supporters of more restrictive immigration policies often argue for more robust border controls and limits on immigration to protect jobs and national security. On the other hand, advocates for more lenient policies emphasize the contributions of immigrants to the economy and society, calling for comprehensive immigration reform and protections for undocumented immigrants.

Gun Violence

Gun violence is another highly polarizing issue, with debates revolving around gun control measures and Second Amendment rights. Supporters of stricter gun control laws advocate for measures such as universal background checks, bans on assault weapons, and limits on high-capacity magazines to reduce gun violence. Those opposed to such measures often argue for the protection of Second Amendment rights and the importance of gun ownership for self-defense and as a safeguard against government tyranny.

LGBTQ+ Rights

LGBTQ+ rights have been a focal point of the cultural divide, particularly regarding issues such as marriage equality, nondiscrimination protections, and transgender rights. Advocates for LGBTQ+ rights emphasize the importance of equal treatment under the law and protections against discrimination based on sexual orientation and gender identity. Opponents may argue for religious freedom exemptions and traditional definitions of marriage and gender, leading to clashes over the scope of civil rights and liberties.

The impact of this cultural divide is significant and multifaceted:

Political Polarization

The cultural divide has contributed to political polarization, increasing ideological and partisan divides between Democrats and Republicans. This polarization often leads to gridlock in Congress and difficulty finding common ground on important policy issues.

Social Fragmentation

The sense of societal disunity and alienation resulting from the cultural divide can lead to social fragmentation. Communities may feel divided along political and cultural lines, making it challenging to find shared values and goals.

Erosion of Trust

The divide has eroded trust in institutions, including government, media, and other societal pillars. Trust in these institutions diminishes when people feel their values and beliefs are not represented or respected.

Echo Chambers and Disinformation

The cultural divide has also led to the rise of echo chambers, where individuals are surrounded by like-minded people and exposed to information reinforcing their beliefs. This can contribute to the spread of misinformation and disinformation, further deepening the divide.

Addressing the cultural divide requires a concerted effort to bridge differences and find common ground:

Dialogue and Understanding

Encouraging respectful dialogue and understanding across ideological lines is essential to bridging the cultural divide. Creating spaces for constructive conversations where diverse perspectives can be heard and respected is crucial.

Empathy and Compassion

Developing empathy and compassion for those with differing viewpoints can help foster understanding and reduce hatred. Recognizing the humanity and dignity of all individuals, regardless of their beliefs, is vital in building bridges.

Education and Media Literacy

Promoting media literacy and critical thinking skills can help combat misinformation and encourage a more informed citizenry. Educating people about the complexities of issues and the nuances of different perspectives can lead to more nuanced discussions.

Policy Solutions

Finding policy solutions that address underlying concerns on both sides of the divide is essential. Compromise and finding common ground on issues such as immigration reform, gun violence prevention, and LGBTQ+ rights can help bridge divides and move toward a more cohesive society.

In conclusion, the cultural divide in the United States presents significant challenges to unity and cohesion. By fostering dialogue, empathy, and understanding and working towards policy solutions that address underlying concerns, the country can work towards bridging these divides and building a more inclusive and harmonious society.

Gender Pay Gap

The gender pay gap remains a significant issue in the United States despite advancements in women's rights and efforts to promote gender equality. This gap refers to the difference in earnings between men and women, with women typically earning less than men for comparable work. Several factors contribute to this persistent disparity:

Occupational Segregation

Women and men often work in different occupations and industries, and women are more likely to be employed in lower-paying fields. This occupational segregation contributes to the gender pay gap, as jobs traditionally held by women tend to pay less than those traditionally held by men. For example, women are overrepresented in fields such as education, healthcare, and administrative support, which tend to have lower average wages compared to male-dominated fields like engineering, finance, and technology.

Discrimination

Discrimination based on gender continues to be a significant factor in the gender pay gap. Women may face pay disparities even when working in the same occupation and with similar levels of education and experience as their male counterparts. This discrimination can manifest in various forms, including unequal pay for equal work, promotion and advancement barriers, and biases in hiring and performance evaluations.

Lack of Family-Friendly Workplace Policies

The absence of supportive policies for work-life balance, such as paid parental leave, flexible work arrangements, and affordable childcare, disproportionately affects women's earnings. Women are more likely to take on caregiving responsibilities for children and elderly family members, which can interrupt their careers and lower earning potential. The lack of family-friendly workplace policies can make it challenging for women to balance work and caregiving responsibilities without sacrificing their careers or financial stability.

Unconscious Bias

Unconscious or implicit biases influencing decision-making and behaviors can contribute to the gender pay gap. These biases may result in women being overlooked for promotions, raises, and leadership opportunities, even when they have the same qualifications and performance as their male counterparts. Stereotypes and assumptions about women's abilities and commitment to work can perpetuate unequal treatment in the workplace.

Negotiation and Salary Transparency

Research suggests that women are less likely than men to negotiate their salaries and benefits, which can contribute to the gender pay gap. Women may also be less aware of their male counterparts' salaries due to a lack of transparency in pay practices. Negotiation skills and access to salary information are essential in closing the gender pay gap, as they empower individuals to advocate for fair compensation.

Addressing the gender pay gap requires a multifaceted approach that addresses these underlying factors:

Policy Changes

Implementing policies to promote pay transparency, strengthen anti-discrimination laws, and mandate equitable pay practices can help reduce the gender pay gap. Laws such as the Lilly Ledbetter Fair Pay Act and state-level pay equity laws aim to address disparities in pay based on gender.

Promoting Diversity and Inclusion

Encouraging diversity and inclusion in the workplace can help combat unconscious bias and create a more equitable work environment. Employers can implement diversity training programs, mentorship opportunities, and inclusive hiring practices to promote equal employee opportunities.

Family-Friendly Policies

Offering paid parental leave, flexible work arrangements and affordable childcare options can help women balance their work and caregiving responsibilities. These policies benefit all employees and contribute to a more productive and engaged workforce.

Education and Awareness

Increasing awareness about the gender pay gap and providing resources for negotiation skills can empower women to advocate for fair compensation. Educational programs in schools and workplaces can also challenge gender stereotypes and promote equal opportunities for men and women.

Corporate Accountability

Holding employers accountable for gender pay disparities through reporting requirements and audits can incentivize companies to address wage gaps. Transparency in pay practices and regular pay equity analyses can help identify and rectify disparities.

In conclusion, the gender pay gap persists in the United States due to a combination of factors, including occupational segregation, discrimination, lack of family-friendly policies, unconscious bias, and negotiation practices. Addressing these factors requires a comprehensive approach involving policy changes, promoting diversity and inclusion, implementing family-friendly policies, educating and empowering individuals, and holding employers accountable. Closing the gender pay gap is not only a matter of economic fairness but also crucial for achieving gender equality and promoting a more just and equitable society.

Global Standing

The United States' global standing has faced challenges in recent years, with criticisms and concerns about its foreign policy decisions, military interventions, and perceived inconsistencies in advocating for democracy and human rights abroad. Several factors have contributed to a tarnished reputation on the world stage:

Foreign Policy Decisions

The U.S. has faced criticism for its foreign policy decisions, including military interventions in countries such as Iraq and Afghanistan. These interventions have been controversial and have led to questions about the effectiveness and legitimacy of U.S. actions on the global stage. Additionally, the U.S.'s approach to international conflicts and crises has drawn criticism from some allies and international organizations.

Perceived Hypocrisy

The U.S. has been accused of hypocrisy in advocating for democracy and human rights abroad while grappling with domestic issues such as racial inequality, gun violence, and political polarization. Critics argue that the U.S.'s actions do not always align with its stated values, leading to skepticism and criticism from other countries.

Erosion of Diplomatic Relationships

The Trump administration's approach to diplomacy, characterized by unilateralism and unpredictability, led to strained relationships with traditional allies and partners. Actions such as imposing tariffs on allies, questioning the value of NATO, and withdrawing from international agreements like the Paris Climate Accord and the Iran nuclear deal created rifts and undermined trust in U.S. leadership.

MAKING AMERICA GREAT ALTOGETHER - CALL TO ACTION

Withdrawal from International Agreements

The U.S.'s withdrawal from key international agreements, such as the Paris Climate Agreement and the Trans-Pacific Partnership (TPP), raised concerns about its commitment to global cooperation and leadership. These withdrawals were seen as setbacks to addressing pressing global challenges, such as climate change and trade liberalization.

Retreat from Multilateralism

The U.S.'s retreat from multilateralism, preferring bilateral negotiations and "America First" policies, has been met with skepticism and concern from other countries. This shift away from multilateral institutions and agreements has raised questions about the U.S.'s willingness to engage in cooperative solutions to global issues.

Trade Disputes

Trade disputes with key allies and trading partners, particularly China, have contributed to tensions and uncertainties in global trade. Tariffs imposed by the U.S. and retaliatory measures from other countries have disrupted supply chains, increased costs for businesses, and raised concerns about the stability of the global economy.

Human Rights Concerns

The U.S.'s handling of human rights issues, both domestically and internationally, has drawn scrutiny. The treatment of migrants and asylum seekers at the U.S.-Mexico border, the response to protests against racial injustice, and controversies over surveillance and privacy have all raised questions about the U.S.'s commitment to human rights principles.

Addressing these challenges to the U.S.'s global standing will require a concerted effort to rebuild diplomatic relationships, reaffirm commitment to international agreements, promote values of democracy and human rights, and engage constructively in multilateral forums. Restoring trust and credibility on the world stage will be essential for the U.S. to regain its position as a respected global leader.

Food Deserts

Food deserts are areas within the United States where residents have limited access to affordable and nutritious food, mainly fresh fruits, vegetables, and whole foods. A lack of grocery stores, supermarkets, and other sources of healthy food options often characterizes these areas. Instead, residents may rely on convenience stores, fast food outlets, and small corner stores that offer mainly processed and unhealthy food choices. Several factors contribute to the existence of food deserts:

Geographic Barriers

In rural areas, food deserts can arise due to long distances to the nearest grocery store or supermarket. Limited public transportation options can make it difficult for residents, particularly those without access to a car, to travel to larger stores where healthier food options are available.

Economic Factors

Low-income neighborhoods are more likely to be food deserts because large grocery chains may be less inclined to open stores in areas with lower purchasing power. The lack of competition in these areas can lead to higher prices for the limited food options available.

Racial and Ethnic Disparities

Food deserts disproportionately affect minority communities, particularly African American and Hispanic neighborhoods. Historical factors such as redlining, which limited investment in specific neighborhoods based on race, have contributed to the concentration of food deserts in these communities.

Limited Availability of Fresh Produce

Even when grocery stores are present in some areas, they may offer limited selections of fresh fruits and vegetables. This can be due to logistical challenges in transporting perishable goods and maintaining freshness in stores with lower foot traffic.

Lack of Nutrition Education

In addition to limited access to healthy food, residents of food deserts may also lack education about nutrition and healthy eating habits. This can perpetuate a cycle of unhealthy food choices and poor health outcomes.

Consequences

The consequences of food deserts are significant and far-reaching:

Health Disparities

Residents of food deserts are more likely to suffer from diet-related health conditions such as obesity, diabetes, and cardiovascular disease. The lack of access to nutritious food contributes to these health outcomes disparities.

Children's Health

Food deserts can have particularly detrimental effects on children's health and development. Limited access to healthy food options can lead to poor academic performance, behavioral issues, and long-term health problems.

Economic Impact

The presence of food deserts can also impact local economies. Without access to healthy food options, residents may spend more on healthcare costs related to diet-related diseases. Additionally, the lack of grocery stores and supermarkets can hinder economic development and job creation.

Efforts to address food deserts include initiatives such as:

Community Gardens and Farmers' Markets

Creating community gardens and supporting farmers' markets in food desert areas can increase access to fresh produce and promote local agriculture.

Mobile Markets and Food Trucks

Mobile markets and food trucks that directly bring fresh produce and healthy food options to neighborhoods can help bridge the gap in food access.

Policy Interventions

Local and state governments can implement policies to incentivize grocery stores to open in food desert areas, such as tax incentives or grants. They can also provide funding for community-led initiatives to address food insecurity.

Education and Outreach

Nutrition education programs can empower residents to make healthier food choices and utilize the available resources more effectively.

Addressing food deserts requires a multifaceted approach that combines policy interventions, community engagement, and support for local initiatives. Improving access to nutritious food can promote better health outcomes and reduce disparities in food access and health.

Disinvestment In Public Education

Disinvestment in public education refers to a trend where funding and resources for public schools in the United States have not kept pace with the needs of students and the demands of a changing education landscape. Several factors contribute to this issue:

Budget Cuts

Many states and local governments have faced budget constraints, leading to cuts in education funding. These cuts often result in reduced staffing, fewer resources for classroom materials, outdated technology, and limited extracurricular programs. As a result, schools may struggle to provide a quality education experience for their students.

Privatization Efforts

Some policymakers and advocates support privatization measures, such as charter schools and voucher programs, as solutions to improve education.

However, these efforts can divert public funds from traditional public schools, further disinvesting the public education system. Critics argue that privatization can exacerbate inequities by siphoning resources from public schools that serve the most vulnerable students.

Standardized Testing Mandates

The emphasis on standardized testing, particularly under the No Child Left Behind Act and the Every Student Succeeds Act, has had unintended consequences. Schools may allocate significant resources to test preparation, administration, and data analysis, often at the expense of other educational priorities. This focus on testing can also create a narrow curriculum that neglects important subjects like art, music, and physical education.

Disparities in Resource Allocation

Inequities in funding distribution between schools can lead to disparities in educational opportunities. Schools in wealthier areas often benefit from higher property tax revenues, resulting in better facilities, more experienced teachers, and access to advanced courses. In contrast, schools in low-income communities may lack adequate resources and struggle to meet the needs of their students.

The consequences of disinvestment in public education are significant:

Quality of Education

Reduced funding can lead to larger class sizes, outdated textbooks, and insufficient support staff. This can impact the quality of instruction and student learning outcomes.

Teacher Retention

Budget cuts may result in layoffs or hiring freezes, leading to a shortage of qualified teachers. Low salaries and limited resources can also contribute to teacher turnover, making maintaining a stable and experienced teaching staff challenging.

Equity

Disinvestment exacerbates inequities in education. Students from low-income backgrounds, students of color, English language learners, and students with disabilities are disproportionately affected by the lack of resources and opportunities.

School Infrastructure

Many public schools across the country have aging infrastructure needing repair and modernization. Disinvestment can prevent schools from addressing these critical needs, such as building maintenance, safety upgrades, and technology updates.

Efforts to address disinvestment in public education include:

Increased Funding

Advocates call for increased state and federal funding for public schools to ensure adequate resources for all students. This includes funding formulas that consider the needs of students in low-income areas.

Equitable Resource Allocation

Policymakers can work to distribute resources more equitably among schools, considering factors such as student demographics and needs.

Reducing Reliance on Standardized Testing

Reevaluating the role of standardized testing in education policy can free up resources for more holistic approaches to student assessment and curriculum development.

Support for Public Schools

Policies that support traditional public schools, such as limiting charter school expansion and voucher programs, can help protect public education from further disinvestment.

By addressing disinvestment in public education, policymakers can work towards providing all students with the resources and opportunities they need to succeed academically and thrive in the future.

Rise Of Hate Crimes

The rise of hate crimes in the United States is a troubling trend that has significant impacts on marginalized communities and society as a whole. Several factors contribute to this rise:

Xenophobia and Racism

Hate crimes often stem from deep-seated prejudices against individuals based on their race, ethnicity, or national origin. Xenophobic and racist ideologies can fuel acts of violence and discrimination, targeting minority communities and perpetuating fear and division.

Bigotry and Intolerance

Hate crimes are driven by intolerance towards individuals who are perceived as different or "other." This intolerance can manifest in acts of vandalism, harassment, or violence against those who do not conform to societal norms or who are part of marginalized groups.

Divisive Rhetoric

Political and social rhetoric that demonizes certain groups or promotes stereotypes can contribute to a climate where hate crimes are more likely to occur. When leaders or influential figures engage in inflammatory speech or endorse discriminatory policies, it can encourage individuals with extremist views.

Online Radicalization

The internet and social media platforms have become breeding grounds for hate speech and radicalization. Extremist groups and individuals use online platforms to spread hateful ideologies, recruit followers, and coordinate acts of violence.

Historical Precedents

The history of systemic discrimination and oppression in the United States has created a legacy of inequality and prejudice. This history, combined with current social and political tensions, can contribute to the perpetuation of hate crimes.

The impacts of the rise in hate crimes are profound:

Fear and Trauma

Victims of hate crimes often experience significant trauma and fear for their safety and the safety of their communities. These incidents can have long-lasting psychological effects and erode individuals' sense of security.

Community Division

Hate crimes can create rifts within communities, pitting groups against each other and undermining social cohesion. Trust between different racial, religious, and ethnic groups can be damaged, making it harder to build inclusive and supportive communities.

Undermining Civil Rights

Hate crimes are not just individual acts of violence; they are attacks on the civil rights and liberties of targeted communities. They send a message of exclusion and intolerance, threatening progress in advancing equality and justice.

Efforts to address the rise of hate crimes include:

Hate Crime Legislation

Strengthening hate crime laws and ensuring they are effectively enforced can send a clear message that these acts will not be tolerated. Enhanced penalties for hate-motivated crimes can serve as a deterrent.

Community Engagement

Building bridges between communities and fostering understanding and empathy can help combat hatred and prejudice. Community organizations, religious institutions, and local leaders are crucial in promoting dialogue and unity.

Education and Awareness

Educating the public about the harms of hate crimes and the importance of diversity and inclusivity is essential. Schools, universities, and community programs can provide education on tolerance, respect, and understanding.

Law Enforcement Training

Training law enforcement officers to recognize and respond to hate crimes effectively is crucial. This includes understanding the motivations behind hate crimes, collecting accurate data, and supporting victims.

Countering Online Extremism

Collaborative efforts between tech companies, law enforcement, and civil society are needed to counter hate speech and extremism online. Platforms must take proactive measures to remove hate content and prevent radicalization.

By addressing the root causes of hate crimes and promoting a culture of inclusivity and acceptance, society can work towards reducing these harmful incidents and creating a safer and more equitable environment for all.

Student Loan Debt Crisis

The student loan debt crisis in the United States has become a significant burden on millions of individuals and families, with far-reaching economic and social implications. Several factors have contributed to the escalation of this crisis:

Rising Tuition Costs

One of the primary drivers of the student loan debt crisis is the steady increase in college tuition costs. Over the past few decades, the cost of attending college has risen much higher than inflation, making higher education increasingly unaffordable for many students and families.

Predatory Lending Practices

Some private lenders have engaged in predatory lending practices, targeting vulnerable students with high-interest loans and misleading terms. These loans often come with unfavorable repayment terms, making it difficult for borrowers to manage their debt after graduation.

Limited Financial Aid

While federal financial aid programs exist to help students afford college, they often fall short of meeting the total cost of tuition, fees, and living expenses. Many students must turn to private loans to bridge the gap, increasing their debt burden.

Lack of Consumer Protection

Unlike other forms of debt, student loans are notoriously difficult to discharge through bankruptcy. Borrowers who face financial hardship may find it challenging to renegotiate their repayment terms or seek relief from overwhelming debt.

Economic Impact

The weight of student loan debt can ripple effect on borrowers' lives and the broader economy. High monthly loan payments limit individuals' ability to save for retirement, buy homes, or start businesses, delaying important milestones and hindering economic growth.

Impact Of Student Loan Debt

The impacts of the student loan debt crisis are significant:

Financial Hardship

Student loan payments consume a significant portion of many borrowers' monthly income. This can lead to financial stress, difficulty covering basic living expenses, and a cycle of debt that is hard to escape.

Limited Opportunities

The burden of student loan debt can limit borrowers' career choices and opportunities. Some may feel pressured to pursue higher-paying jobs rather than following their passions or entering public service careers with lower salaries.

Wealth Inequality

The student loan debt crisis disproportionately affects low-income and minority borrowers, exacerbating wealth inequality. These individuals often have fewer resources to repay their loans. They may face higher interest rates due to factors like credit history.

Impact on Mental Health

The stress and anxiety of managing significant student loan debt can take a toll on borrowers' mental health. Depression, anxiety, and feelings of hopelessness are common among those struggling with debt.

Efforts to address the student loan debt crisis include:

Loan Forgiveness Programs - Some federal programs offer loan forgiveness for borrowers who work in public service or certain professions. However, these programs often have strict eligibility requirements and limited availability.

Income-Driven Repayment Plans

Federal student loans offer income-driven repayment plans, which cap monthly payments based on borrowers' income and family size. These plans can provide relief for borrowers with low incomes.

Advocacy for Policy Changes

There are ongoing efforts to push for policy changes at the federal level, such as expanding loan forgiveness programs, reducing interest rates, and increasing funding for Pell Grants and other forms of financial aid.

Financial Literacy Education

Educating students and families about the implications of student loan debt and how to make informed borrowing decisions can help prevent future crises. Schools, colleges, and community organizations play a role in providing this education.

Addressing the student loan debt crisis requires a multifaceted approach that addresses the root causes of rising tuition costs, predatory lending practices, and limited financial aid. By providing relief for current borrowers and implementing policies to prevent future borrowers from falling into excessive debt, policymakers can work towards a more equitable and accessible higher education system.

Crisis In Affordable Housing

The crisis in affordable housing in the United States has reached alarming levels, impacting millions of individuals and families across the country. Several factors contribute to this crisis:

Stagnant Wages

While housing costs have continued to rise, wages for many Americans have remained stagnant or have not kept pace with housing costs. This means that a more significant portion of individuals' and families' incomes goes towards housing, leaving less for other essential expenses.

Gentrification

In many urban areas, gentrification has led to the displacement of low-income residents as neighborhoods undergo redevelopment and property values increase. This can result in rising rents and housing costs, making it difficult for long-time residents to afford to remain in their homes.

Insufficient Government Investment

There has been a lack of sufficient government investment in affordable housing programs and initiatives. Federal funding for programs like public housing, Section 8 vouchers, and Low-Income Housing Tax Credits has not kept up with the growing need, leading to long waiting lists and inadequate housing options.

Limited Availability of Affordable Housing Units

There is a nationwide shortage of affordable housing units, particularly for highly low-income individuals and families. This shortage is exacerbated by converting affordable units into market-rate housing and the lack of new construction of affordable housing.

Homelessness

The lack of affordable housing has contributed to a rise in homelessness in many communities. Individuals and families who cannot afford housing are forced to live in shelters, on the streets, or in inadequate and overcrowded living situations.

The impacts of the affordable housing crisis are far-reaching:

Housing Insecurity

Many households are burdened by housing costs, spending much of their income on rent or mortgage payments. This leaves little room for savings, emergencies, or other basic needs.

Homelessness

The lack of affordable housing options has led to a rise in homelessness, with individuals and families struggling to find stable and safe places to live. Homelessness has profound impacts on physical and mental health, employment opportunities, and overall well-being.

Health Disparities

Inadequate and unstable housing can lead to health disparities, as individuals living in substandard housing are more likely to experience poor health outcomes. Lack of access to safe and affordable housing contributes to chronic stress, respiratory illnesses, and other health issues.

Educational Challenges

Children living in unstable housing often face school challenges, including frequent moves, disruptions in education, and difficulty concentrating. This can have long-term consequences for their academic achievement and future opportunities.

Efforts to address the affordable housing crisis include:

Expanding Affordable Housing Programs

There are calls to expand funding for affordable housing programs, such as Section 8 vouchers and public housing, to meet the growing need.

Increasing Minimum Wage

Advocates argue that increasing the minimum wage to a livable wage would help individuals and families afford housing without being cost-burdened.

Promoting Mixed-Income Housing

Building mixed-income housing developments can help create more diverse and inclusive communities while providing affordable options for low-income residents.

Zoning and Land Use Policies

Some cities reevaluate zoning and land use policies to encourage affordable housing development and prevent displacement.

Homelessness Prevention Programs

Investing in homelessness prevention programs, such as rapid rehousing and supportive services, can help individuals and families avoid homelessness and stabilize their housing situations.

Addressing the affordable housing crisis requires a comprehensive and coordinated effort at the federal, state, and local levels. By investing in affordable housing, increasing wages, and implementing policies to prevent displacement, policymakers can work towards ensuring that all individuals and families have access to safe, stable, and affordable housing.

Exploitation Of Agricultural Workers

The exploitation of agricultural workers in the United States, including farmworkers and migrant laborers, is a pervasive issue that has long-lasting impacts on individuals and communities. Several factors contribute to this exploitation:

Low Wages

Agricultural workers often earn low wages well below the federal minimum wage. Many are paid based on piece rates or the amount of produce they harvest, which can result in unpredictable and inadequate earnings. The low wages make it difficult for agricultural workers to support themselves and their families, leading to financial insecurity.

Unsafe Working Conditions

Agricultural work is inherently hazardous, with exposure to pesticides, heat stress, and heavy machinery posing significant risks to workers' health and safety. Many agricultural workers do not receive proper training on safety protocols, and employers may fail to provide adequate protective equipment. This lack of safety measures puts workers at risk of injuries and illnesses.

Lack of Legal Protections

Agricultural workers are often excluded from basic labor protections afforded to workers in other industries. This includes exemptions from overtime pay, limited access to collective bargaining rights, and exclusion from federal labor laws like the National Labor Relations Act. This lack of legal protections leaves agricultural workers vulnerable to exploitation and abuse.

Wage Theft

Wage theft, which includes not paying workers for all hours worked or withholding wages altogether, is a common issue in the agricultural industry. Some employers may also misclassify workers as independent contractors to avoid providing benefits and complying with labor laws.

Limited Access to Healthcare

Many agricultural workers lack access to healthcare and essential medical services. This is particularly concerning given the hazardous nature of their work and the increased risk of injuries and illnesses. Migrant workers, in particular, face barriers to accessing healthcare due to language barriers, immigration status, and lack of insurance coverage.

Housing Insecurity

Migrant agricultural workers often live in substandard and overcrowded housing provided by employers. These housing conditions are often unsanitary, lack basic amenities, and fail to meet health and safety standards. Workers may also face threats of eviction or retaliation if they raise concerns about their living conditions.

The impacts of the exploitation of agricultural workers are profound:

Health Consequences

Unsafe working conditions and lack of access to healthcare contribute to higher rates of injuries, illnesses, and chronic health conditions among agricultural workers. This includes respiratory problems from pesticide exposure, heat-related illnesses, and musculoskeletal injuries.

Financial Hardship

Low wages and wage theft leave agricultural workers struggling to make ends meet and support themselves and their families. Many live in poverty or near-poverty conditions, with limited opportunities for economic advancement.

MAKING AMERICA GREAT ALTOGETHER - CALL TO ACTION

Legal Vulnerability

The lack of legal protections makes agricultural workers vulnerable to exploitation and abuse by employers. Fear of retaliation or deportation prevents many workers from reporting violations or seeking justice.

Intersecting Injustices

Many agricultural workers are part of marginalized communities, including immigrants, people of color, and undocumented individuals. This intersectionality compounds the challenges they face and exacerbates their vulnerability to exploitation.

Efforts to address the exploitation of agricultural workers include:

Improving Labor Protections - Advocates call for expanding labor protections to cover agricultural workers, including minimum wage laws, overtime pay, and the right to organize and bargain collectively.

Enhancing Workplace Safety - Stricter enforcement of safety regulations and providing training on safety practices can help reduce injuries and illnesses among agricultural workers.

Healthcare Access - Increasing access to affordable healthcare and culturally competent medical services is essential for addressing the health needs of agricultural workers.

Ending Wage Theft - Enforcing laws against wage theft and providing avenues for workers to report violations without fear of retaliation is crucial to combating this issue.

Housing Standards—Implementing and enforcing housing standards for agricultural workers can ensure safe and adequate living conditions.

Education and Outreach - Providing education and outreach programs to inform agricultural workers about their rights, available resources, and how to report violations can empower them to advocate for themselves.

Addressing the exploitation of agricultural workers requires a multi-faceted approach that addresses systemic inequalities, improves working conditions, and provides essential protections and resources to ensure the dignity and well-being of these essential workers.

Environmental Injustice

Environmental injustice refers to the unequal distribution of environmental benefits and burdens, where marginalized communities bear a disproportionate burden of environmental pollution and hazards. Several factors contribute to environmental injustice in the United States:

Environmental Racism

Environmental racism refers to the intentional or unintentional targeting of communities of color for the siting of hazardous waste facilities, industrial pollution, and other environmental hazards. Historically, discriminatory practices in housing, zoning, and land-use policies have resulted in communities of color being located near industrial facilities, landfills, and toxic waste sites. This exposes residents to higher levels of pollution and health risks.

Discriminatory Land-Use Policies

Land-use policies and zoning decisions often result in the placement of polluting facilities in low-income neighborhoods and communities of color. These communities may lack the political power and resources to resist these sitings, leading to a concentration of environmental hazards in their neighborhoods.

Lack of Regulatory Enforcement

Inadequate enforcement of environmental regulations and lax oversight allow polluting industries to operate without sufficient accountability. This leads to violations of environmental standards and exacerbates environmental pollution in vulnerable communities.

Cumulative Impacts

Marginalized communities often face multiple sources of pollution, known as cumulative impacts. These include exposure to air pollution from nearby highways, industrial emissions, contaminated water sources, and toxic waste sites. The combined effects of these pollutants can have severe health consequences for residents.

Health Disparities

Environmental injustice contributes to health disparities in affected communities. Residents may suffer from higher rates of respiratory illnesses, cardiovascular diseases, cancer, and other health conditions linked to environmental pollution. Children and pregnant women are particularly vulnerable to the adverse effects of exposure to environmental toxins.

Limited Access to Green Spaces

Many marginalized communities also lack access to green spaces and recreational areas, further exacerbating environmental inequities. Green spaces provide numerous health benefits, including improved mental health and reduced stress. However, communities with limited resources often lack these amenities.

Displacement and Gentrification

Environmental injustices can also lead to displacement and gentrification. As areas become more polluted and undesirable for living, residents may be forced to relocate. Conversely, as neighborhoods are revitalized and property values increase, long-time residents may be priced out of their communities.

Efforts to address environmental injustice include:

Environmental Justice Advocacy

Grassroots organizations and environmental justice advocates work to raise awareness about environmental injustice, empower affected communities, and push for policy changes. These groups often engage in community organizing, education, and direct action to address environmental inequities.

Policy Reforms

Advocates call for more vigorous enforcement of environmental regulations, improved land-use policies, and increased transparency in decision-making processes. This includes measures to ensure vulnerable communities have a voice in environmental decision-making.

Health Equity

Addressing health disparities related to environmental pollution requires targeted interventions, such as increased access to healthcare, environmental health education, and health screenings for affected communities.

Community-Based Solutions

Engaging communities in the development of solutions is essential. This includes supporting community-led initiatives for clean energy, sustainable development, and green infrastructure projects that benefit residents and improve environmental quality.

Legal Protections

Advocates also push for legal protections that prevent environmental racism and ensure all communities have equal access to clean air, water, and a healthy environment. This includes civil rights laws and environmental justice legislation at the local, state, and federal levels.

By addressing environmental injustice, policymakers, advocates, and communities can work together to create healthier and more equitable environments for all residents, regardless of race or socioeconomic status.

By acknowledging and confronting these issues, the United States can foster a more inclusive, just, and sustainable future for all its citizens. This requires collective action, policy reforms, community empowerment, and a commitment to upholding human rights, dignity, and social justice for every individual. Ultimately, building a more equitable society requires ongoing efforts to dismantle systems of oppression, challenge inequality, and create opportunities for all people to thrive and fulfill their potential.

The Need For Unity And Collaboration

Amidst the intricate web of challenges that define America's current state, a resounding call for unity and collaboration emerges as a beacon of hope and a pathway toward transformative change. This call is a rhetorical gesture and a pragmatic response to the interwoven complexities that demand a collective effort to navigate.

Socio-economic inequality, healthcare disparities, environmental degradation, and social and racial tensions show that no single individual or group has all the answers. These multifaceted and deeply entrenched challenges require a comprehensive approach that draws upon diverse stakeholders' insights, expertise, and resources.

Unity and collaboration offer a way forward by leveraging the collective strengths of the American people. We can pool our talents, perspectives, and resources to tackle these challenges head-on by coming together across ideological divides, political affiliations, and cultural differences.

But unity is not just about agreeing on everything; it's about finding common ground and working towards shared goals. It's about recognizing that, despite our differences, we are all in this together and that our collective well-being depends on the well-being of others.

Collaboration, likewise, is about more than just cooperation; it's about genuine partnership and mutual respect. It's about listening to diverse voices, valuing different perspectives, and finding creative solutions that benefit everyone.

The urgency of our challenges underscores the need for unity and collaboration. These problems cannot be solved by one person or one group alone. They require a concerted effort from all sectors of society—government, business, academia, civil society, and the community at large.

But perhaps most importantly, unity and collaboration offer a vision of hope in a time of uncertainty. They remind us that, despite our differences, we share a common humanity and destiny. They inspire us to believe that we can overcome even the most significant challenges and build a better future for ourselves and future generations.

In the puzzle of progress, unity and collaboration are the missing pieces that bring the picture into focus. By embracing these values and working together toward a common purpose, we can chart a course toward a stronger, more resilient, and more compassionate America for all.

Bridge The Divides

Unity is a crucial antidote to the deep divides that have emerged in America's social and political landscape. The polarization that grips the nation threatens to paralyze progress and erode the bonds that hold society together, fostering an environment of hate and distrust.

At the heart of this polarization lie ideological differences that seem to grow wider by the day. Political affiliations, cultural identities, and social values often serve as barriers that separate us from one another, fueling an "us versus them" mentality that breeds hostility and resentment.

Yet, amidst this sea of discord, unity emerges as a powerful force for change. It calls upon us to transcend our ideological differences and instead focus on what unites us as Americans. It challenges us to seek out common ground, to listen to diverse perspectives, and to find solutions that benefit all members of society.

Embracing unity means recognizing that America's strength lies in its diversity. Our nation is a tapestry of cultures, beliefs, and backgrounds, each thread contributing to the rich fabric of American society. It's this diversity that gives America its vitality, resilience, and capacity for innovation and progress.

But unity is not just a feel-good sentiment; it's a practical imperative. It allows us to come together in times of crisis to overcome challenges that no single individual or group could face alone. It enables us to build bridges across divides and forge partnerships based on mutual respect and understanding.

In the puzzle of progress, unity is like the glue that holds the pieces together, ensuring we can move forward as a cohesive and resilient society. By embracing unity and celebrating our diversity, we can transcend the polarization that threatens to tear us apart and build a stronger, more inclusive America for all.

Collaboration

Collaboration is a powerful amplifier of strength by fostering a collective approach to problem-solving. America's challenges are multifaceted and complex, requiring diverse perspectives and expertise to unravel their intricacies. Collaboration catalyzes innovative solutions that address the root causes of these challenges by bringing together individuals, communities, and institutions.

Collaboration is about leveraging each participant's unique strengths and insights to create something more significant than the sum of its parts. It's about recognizing that no single person or entity holds all the answers and that by working together, we can tap into a wealth of knowledge, creativity, and resources.

Collaboration offers a way forward to facing challenges like socioeconomic inequality, healthcare disparities, environmental degradation, and social and racial tensions. It allows us to pool our talents, perspectives, and resources to tackle these issues from multiple angles, uncovering new insights and approaches.

But collaboration is more than just cooperation; it's about building relationships based on trust, mutual respect, and shared goals. It's about fostering an environment where everyone feels valued and empowered to contribute their ideas and expertise.

Collaboration brings together diverse stakeholders and opens the door to innovative solutions that address the root causes of our most pressing challenges. It encourages us to think outside the box, challenge assumptions, and embrace new ways of thinking and working together.

In the puzzle of progress, collaboration is like the missing piece that completes the picture. By harnessing the collective power of individuals, communities, and institutions, we can unlock new possibilities and create a more just, equitable, and sustainable future for all.

Politics

In politics, unity and collaboration are pivotal pillars for transcending partisan divides and fostering effective governance. Making America Great Altogether underscores the critical importance of politicians working across party lines to enact meaningful and sustainable policies addressing the nation's pressing issues. It envisions a political landscape where collaboration precedes polarization, leading to legislation that genuinely serves the nation's interests.

At its core, this vision of unity in politics recognizes that no single party or ideology monopolizes good ideas. By bringing together lawmakers from across the political spectrum, we can tap into a broader range of perspectives and expertise, fostering innovative solutions to complex challenges.

Moreover, political collaboration is not just about reaching a compromise for compromise's sake. It's about finding common ground based on shared values and principles and working together towards common goals. This approach requires listening to opposing viewpoints, engaging in respectful dialogue, and prioritizing the greater good over narrow partisan interests.

Politicians can break free from the gridlock and dysfunction that have characterized the political landscape in recent years by transcending partisan divides. Instead of focusing on scoring political points or obstructing the other party, lawmakers can come together to tackle the pressing issues facing the nation, from healthcare and education to infrastructure and climate change.

In this vision, collaboration doesn't just lead to better policy outcomes; it also helps to rebuild trust and confidence in government institutions. When lawmakers are willing to work together in the nation's best interests, it sends a powerful message to the American people that their elected officials can put aside their differences and govern effectively.

Ultimately, Making America Great Altogether emphasizes unity and political collaboration as lofty ideals and essential ingredients for a healthy democracy.

By fostering a political culture that values cooperation over confrontation, we can create a more responsive, inclusive, and effective government that truly serves the needs of all Americans.

Economically

Economically, unity is a driving force for addressing socio-economic inequalities and fostering a more inclusive economy. By promoting a shared commitment to equity and opportunity, collaborative efforts between businesses, government, and communities can lead to initiatives that uplift marginalized groups, create equal opportunities, and build a more robust, more resilient economy for all.

At its core, this approach to economic unity recognizes that socio-economic inequalities are not just a moral issue but also an economic one. When large segments of the population are left behind, it weakens the overall economy, stifles growth, and undermines the nation's long-term prosperity. By addressing these inequalities head-on, we can unlock the full potential of all Americans and create a more vibrant and dynamic economy.

Collaboration between businesses, government, and communities is essential for driving meaningful change. Businesses create jobs, drive innovation, and stimulate economic growth. By adopting inclusive hiring practices, investing in workforce development programs, and supporting minority-owned businesses, companies can help to uplift marginalized communities and create pathways to economic opportunity.

The government also has a critical role to play in promoting economic unity. Through policies and programs that promote access to education, healthcare, and affordable housing, the government can help level the playing field and ensure that all Americans have the opportunity to succeed. Additionally, the government can work to remove barriers to economic mobility, such as discriminatory lending practices or zoning laws that perpetuate segregation.

Communities are the heart and soul of the economy, and their involvement is essential for driving sustainable change. By fostering partnerships between businesses, government, and grassroots organizations, communities can leverage their collective resources and expertise to address local challenges and create economic opportunities for all residents.

In the puzzle of economic progress, unity is like the missing piece that unlocks the economy's full potential. By promoting collaboration and a shared commitment to addressing socioeconomic inequalities, we can build a more inclusive economy that benefits everyone, regardless of their background or circumstances.

Unity And Collaboration

At its core, the imperative for unity and collaboration stems from recognizing a shared destiny among all Americans. The challenges America faces today, whether socio-economic inequalities, healthcare disparities, environmental degradation, or social and racial tensions, are not isolated to specific regions or demographics; they affect the entire nation. Embracing unity entails acknowledging this interconnectedness and realizing that the fate of one part of the country inevitably impacts the whole. It means understanding that we are all inextricably linked and that our collective well-being depends on our ability to work together towards common goals.

In American society's puzzle, unity is the glue that holds the pieces together, ensuring we can weather storms and overcome obstacles as one cohesive unit. It's a recognition that our destinies are intertwined and that our strength lies in our ability to support and uplift one another.

By embracing unity, we can build a more resilient and harmonious society better equipped to face the challenges of the present and the uncertainties of the future. It means moving beyond narrow self-interest and embracing a broader vision of collective progress and prosperity.

Ultimately, unity is not just a lofty ideal; it's a practical necessity. In a world of increasing complexity and interdependence, working together and finding common ground is essential for tackling our nation's pressing issues. Coming together as one can create a brighter future for ourselves and our generations.

The Call For Unity And Collaboration

The call for unity and collaboration is not a naive aspiration but a pragmatic and necessary response to the complexities of America's current state. It recognizes that the challenges we face are multifaceted and deeply entrenched and that addressing them requires a concerted effort from all sectors of society. It's a rallying cry for a nation to come together, learn from its diverse history, and collectively shape a future that reflects the values of unity, collaboration, and shared prosperity.

This call is rooted in a profound understanding of the interconnectedness of our challenges and the power of collective action to effect meaningful change. It acknowledges that no single individual or group holds all the answers and that by working together, we can tap into a wealth of knowledge, creativity, and resources to tackle even the most daunting challenges.

Moreover, this call recognizes the richness and diversity of America's history and culture. It's an acknowledgment that our nation's strength lies in its ability to embrace and celebrate our differences and draw upon our shared experiences' wisdom to forge a better future for all.

But perhaps most importantly, this call is a reminder that unity and collaboration are not just lofty ideals but practical imperatives. In a world of increasing complexity and uncertainty, the ability to come together and find common ground is essential for navigating the challenges. By embracing unity and collaboration, we can build a stronger, more resilient society better equipped to tackle the pressing issues of our time.

In the puzzle of progress, unity and collaboration are like the missing pieces that bring the picture into focus. We can create a more just, equitable, and prosperous future for all by embracing these values and working together towards a common purpose.

Don't miss out!

Visit the website below and you can sign up to receive emails whenever Adrian Rocquecliffe publishes a new book. There's no charge and no obligation.

https://books2read.com/r/B-A-LUNRB-ZEPED

BOOKS 2 READ

Connecting independent readers to independent writers.

Did you love *Making America Great Altogether - Call to Action*? Then you should read *Trump's Vision of MAGA- The Fallacy*[1] by Adrian Rocquecliffe!

[2]

"Trump's Vision of MAGA - The Fallacy," book of Making America Great Altogether, delves into a riveting critique of contemporary American politics. With sharp wit and incisive analysis, this book challenges the notion of a unified vision for America's greatness. Meticulous examination unravels the puzzle pieces of policies, rhetoric, and actions, revealing the fractures beneath the surface of the supposed MAGA movement. Prepare to confront uncomfortable truths and rethink the narrative surrounding America's path forward. Whether you're a seasoned political observer or a curious citizen seeking clarity, "Trump's Vision of MAGA - The Fallacy" is essential for understanding modern American society's complexities.

Read more at https://www.makingamericagreataltogether.us/adrian_rocquecliffe.

---

1. https://books2read.com/u/b6JkQ0

2. https://books2read.com/u/b6JkQ0

Also by Adrian Rocquecliffe

Making America Great Altogether - Call to Action
Trump's Vision of MAGA- The Fallacy
Extra! Extra! Read All About It
Trump's Insurrection of the US Capitol
How Well do you Know Your Candidate?
Trumpisms: Decoding the Rhetoric of Disruption
The Republican Agenda: Undoing 200 Years of Democracy for a Dictatorship
Under the Iron Flag: A Family's Battle for Survival and Justice in Trump's America
Complimentary Orchiectomy with First Sexual Offense: Starting at the Top
The Gulf of America: Trump's Vision for a United Continent
Project 2026 USA: We the People, For the People, By the People

Watch for more at https://www.makingamericagreataltogether.us/adrian_rocquecliffe.

About the Author

Adrian Rocquecliffe's journey from a young boy navigating cultural divides to a successful entrepreneur and visionary leader exemplifies the American dream. His dedication to improving the country for future generations is a testament to his belief in the power of unity and collaboration. As he continues his work with "Making America Great Altogether," Adrian remains hopeful that his efforts will contribute to a better, more inclusive America when he retires.

Read more at https://www.makingamericagreataltogether.us/adrian_rocquecliffe.

About the Publisher

Writers Sidekick Publishing is a key part of the Writers Sidekick Resource Hub. Writers Sidekick Publishing specializes in publishing anthologies that welcome submissions from both new and established authors, providing a platform to showcase their work and contribute to the literary world. Additionally, it produces exclusive books tailored to the needs of the Writers Sidekick Resource Hub community.